Lively Learning

Using the Arts to Teach the K–8 Curriculum

Linda Crawford

ISBN 978-1-892989-11-6

Library of Congress Control Number: 2004101361

Photographs: Jo Devlin, Peter Wrenn, Usry Alleyne

Illustrations: Elizabeth Crawford (pp. 29–36, 39, 163), Usry Alleyne (pp. 37–38)

Cover and book design: Woodward Design

NORTHEAST FOUNDATION FOR CHILDREN, INC.
85 Avenue A, Suite 204
P. O. Box 718
Turners Falls, MA 01376-0718
800-360-6332
www.responsiveclassroom.org

13 12 11 10   9 8 7 6 5 4 3

For the children

Acknowledgements

Many contributed to this book. It draws from fifteen years of arts-integration workshops for teachers, which I and my artist-teacher daughter, Elizabeth, developed. She also contributed much of the chapter on drawing and served as a sounding board and spark for many other elements of the book. It is my great pleasure and honor to collaborate with her.

Other support came from dozens of arts-integrating teachers who opened their classrooms to me. Some of the most patient and loyal among them were Marilynn O'Donnell; Lisa Boland Blake; Elizabeth Hagedorn; Erin Klug; Allison Forester; Jane Gravender; Marilyn Kammueller; Stephanie Bensen; Karen Randall; Kandace Logan; my daughter, Jessica Crawford; Jill Reshanov; Margaret Burke; Meri Gauthier; Mary Ann Fabel; Sharon Greaves; Mary Spohr; Jeremy Nellis; Dr. Terrance Kwame-Ross; Ellen Shulman; Patricia Pendleton; Annelise Aaro; and Usry Alleyne. These teachers gave direct help to this project, along with many others who continue to inspire and inform me with their commitment to engaging children in academics through the arts.

Helen Stub, my steadfast librarian friend, chased after books, articles, and wayward citations, and worked on the resource list.

Lynn Bechtel, editor and project manager at Northeast Foundation for Children, spent many hours bringing the book from manuscript to finished product—organizing content, preserving the focus, and managing the production with great care and integrity.

Roxann Kriete, executive director of Northeast Foundation for Children, was the person who believed enough in the importance of the subject to give the go-ahead for the book.

Mary Beth Forton, director of publications at Northeast Foundation for Children, helped me keep my eye on what was most important—the usefulness of the book to the busy classroom teachers for whom it was written.

In addition, the following people played an invaluable part in the production of the book:

Allen Woods, who read the initial manuscript and mapped out a way to organize the material that kept both the passion and the purpose clear;

Alice Yang and Sarah Fiarman, who also read an early version of the book and whose questions and comments helped guide revision;

Janice Gadaire-Fleuriel, who copyedited and proofread the final manuscript, keeping a careful eye on all the small details;

Leslie and Jeff Woodward, who created a book design that is both appealing and useful.

Most of all, I thank my partner, Jo Devlin. Knowing that she would be the first reader of every chapter, I stuck to the truth, wrote from the heart, and looked for the light moments in the classroom that give us courage and joy. She was the photographer for most of the pictures in the book as well, and as she so often does in life, she managed to catch the action and make light where there was none before.

These people were crucial to the writing of this book, and in full awareness of that, and in gratitude, I thank them.

Table of Contents

Arts Throughout the Day

The hallway outside Marilynn O'Donnell's primary grade classroom in Minneapolis is covered with self-portraits. Inside, everyone's "Hopes and Dreams for the Year" sail along high on a wall in bright balloon shapes. Another corner displays interviews the children have done with people in their community, complete with drawings of the "Police Commander" and other notables. A table holds dioramas showing the varieties of weather in Minnesota, with figures standing under umbrellas and in the snow. There is a clothesline strung along a wall, filled with paper bag masks (inspired by the traveling exhibit of Latin American masks the school is hosting) and labeled drawings of children doing things with an adult in their lives: "Aunt Beki—I had a sleepover with her." The room belongs to the children and displays what they know and what they imagine.

At eight in the morning, children seated at tables around the room are using number stories to practice computation skills. Marilynn has given them a sample story, but some are making up their own stories, illustrating them, and writing the number sentences that represent them: "Harry caught a fish. Then Harry caught another fish. 1 + 1 = 2." The stories and drawings are both imaginative and accurate, and the children informally share them with each other.

During their morning meeting, the children engage in a spirited round of *Bobo She Wattin Tattin,* a song-chant, hand-jive game played for decades on the streets and playgrounds of America. After the meeting, the seven-year-olds gather on the rug and review with Marilynn how they'll show their understanding of the *George and Martha* books they've read recently: they could write a poem about *George and Martha;* act out one of the stories from their book; or write their own *George and Martha* story and illustrate it. The children get to work, first filling out planning sheets, which Marilynn reviews and approves.

Towards the end of the morning, Marilynn gathers the children to do some reflection on the morning. But first, she puts on a CD and chooses six-year-old Jeffrey to lead the group in a movement routine, one of several the class knows that allow them to move when that is what their muscles and bones and brains require. After the brief movement routine, they are able to think and talk about the work of the morning.

In the afternoon, Marilynn and the children read aloud together and then the fifth and sixth grade learning buddies arrive. Pairs of older and younger children settle in to read, solve problems with math manipulatives, or write together.

As this glimpse into Marilynn's classroom illustrates, children learn eagerly and well in an arts-enriched learning environment. Drawing, storytelling, singing, theater, and movement are naturally appealing to children, and incorporating these art forms into daily curriculum work sweetens the exploration of just about any subject.

Geography Comes Alive

I learned this lesson well when I was in elementary school more than fifty years ago. Geography was a discipline that I struggled with. I found it very hard to keep all those place names and locations straight. The only thing I could do was start memorizing. I tried to picture the fifty states in relation to each other, but they insisted on getting mixed up (still do). "Is Tennessee on top of Arkansas?" I'm likely to ask.

Then one day, when I had only about half the states correct, my fifth grade teacher announced that we were now going to study the land forms of our continent—how the mountains and valleys and plains configured themselves from New York to California. Oh, groan!

She continued, "Everyone will have the chance to show us the landforms, but each person can decide how." The magic words—"decide how"! My "how" was a papier-mâché relief map that I made with two other students. We shaped the Rocky Mountains and the Appalachians, long chunky progressions from north to south, one each near the east and west coasts. We made the Rockies rough and pointy and high—new mountains. We made the Appalachians rounded to show their age. We painted the map brown, green, and blue—we wanted it to be beautiful as well as accurate. It took up four desk tops on its huge piece of cardboard.

And now, if I shut my eyes, I can see clearly the topography of the United States, two long strands of brown bumps enclosing a big plain of green with a bright blue ribbon of a river running through it. That colorful, visual image still provides the context for all the details I have learned since about the geography of North America.

The arts offer multiple, effective ways to explore and understand concepts, master content, memorize facts, solve problems, and express important thoughts and deep feelings about the world. They make facts and figures lively and help the abstract take on shape and color. Children are likely to remember and use what they have learned with such zest.

In this book I present ways to teach the core curriculum and strengthen learning using five main arts media—visual arts, music, movement, theater, and poetry. I suggest practical strategies for getting comfortable with the art forms, for introducing the various art forms to students, and for integrating the arts into every subject area.

But Don't I Have to Be Artistic to Teach Through the Arts?

The answer is no. I did not write this book for artists, or even for art or music or dance teachers, although it stands at the intersection between their work and the work of the classroom teacher. While some arts specialists have tried out the ideas presented here and have found rich possibilities for integrating other media into their teaching and for working more productively with non-specialists, I wrote this book for the K–8 classroom teacher.

For almost twenty-five years through my nonprofit organization, Origins, I have worked with teachers and children to build strong learning communities. One of the ways I do this is by helping teachers integrate arts media into classrooms and learning. I have found that, given the desire, the proper tools, and some guidance, even those who have little experience with art forms can use the arts to teach more effectively. The only prerequisite is that the teachers be willing to learn alongside their students.

None of what I suggest here is meant to supplant the disciplined approach to an art form best provided by an expert in that form. Whenever financially feasible, inviting guest artists, musicians, actors, dancers, and poets into the classroom is a powerful spur to arts development and learning in general. Use them when you can. If you are fortunate enough to have an arts specialist on your staff, buddy up with her or him.

Move at Your Own Pace

Throughout this book you will find many suggestions for places and ways to integrate art forms into daily lessons, but it is important that you proceed with arts-integration at your own pace. Sometimes a sample lesson will contain a number of arts experiences. But these are suggestions only. You can go slowly, gradually inserting arts opportunities here and there. And even when you are fully engaged in arts-integration, you will be offering as many or more non-arts as arts options. The idea is not to drop all other ways of learning, but to become comfortable and adept at offering frequent opportunities for children to learn through drawing, singing, movement, drama, and poetry writing.

I wrote this book knowing that teachers are pressed for time: they need to prepare children to take standardized tests of information-based basic skills; shape learning goals around high standards as described by the state; and work to address the content, concepts, and skills described in their district curriculum guides. It's a constant challenge to find the time and the methods to include frequent arts-related experiences in schedules already packed with required curriculum. It can be done, however, in lots of little ways as well as with big projects. This book is not about teaching more, but about teaching differently. It is about linking up what we want to teach each day with *how* we teach it so that the learning will shine.

CHAPTER 1

Accessible and Alive: Six Good Reasons for Using the Arts to Teach Curriculum

The traditional way to transmit knowledge within many tribal communities was for older generations to take on the job of teaching the children. For example, in the old days very young Inuit girls learned to use the razor-sharp woman's knife, the ulu, by watching their mothers and grandmothers cut meat, trim lamp wicks, cut seal or caribou skins, even cut their hair. Boys watched their fathers and grandfathers use the longer man's knife to butcher a walrus or cut skins into strips for dog harnesses. The teaching took place naturally and quietly, part of the rhythm of daily life. All the life-skills in early tribal communities— weaving, pottery-making, carving, hunting, sewing, etc.—were passed on largely by example and learned through trial and error. Necessity was the test, survival the reward.

We are still teaching the disciplines our children need to thrive, but in a far different world. We teach them language, because they need to become good communicators in speech and in writing; reading, so that they can learn on their own what other people know; mathematics, so they can operate successfully in the concrete world of making and exchanging; geography, history, science— they all seem important to success.

But if our goal is for children to become knowledgeable, critical thinkers who are good at solving problems, we need to pay attention to the "how" of teaching. We need to stimulate curiosity. We need to teach children how to analyze problems on their own and let them practice solving those problems creatively. We need to help them energetically absorb, remember, and apply skills and knowledge. And the arts can help us do this.

There are six powerful reasons for integrating the arts into the daily curriculum:

1. The arts make content more accessible.

2. The arts encourage joyful, active learning.

3. The arts help students make and express personal connections to content.

4. The arts help children understand and express abstract concepts.

5. The arts stimulate higher-level thinking.

6. The arts build community and help children develop collaborative work skills.

Reason 1:
The Arts Make Content More Accessible

Over the years when I've asked teachers how they learn most effectively, a few have said they learn by listening to new information. But far more have said they learn best if they see something visually or get a chance to try it out. Apparently most of us learn best by looking, talking, making, or moving, or by teaching someone else, and so do the children in our classrooms.

Some students' first love and first talent is talking rather than writing. Teachers can help these students practice writing skills by channeling the talking into oral storytelling, which then leads to writing down the stories and editing the written versions.

For students who are visual learners, drawing might provide a doorway to writing. I sometimes ask first graders to draw a picture to represent a special word they are thinking about when they come into the classroom in the morning. If the word is "stomachache," for example, and the picture of a sad face appears on the page, a sentence such as "I threw up" may follow quickly. The sequence of idea-to-picture-to-words is a natural one.

Visual learners might also use drawing to work out story problems in math: "If Corey buys six packages of potato chips, gives one each to three of his friends, and eats one at lunch, how many will he have left?" Amanda can draw the six packages of chips, use arrows to show the transfer of three of them, cross out the fourth, and then count how many are left.

Some children learn best when they engage their whole bodies. These kinesthetic learners might want to act out a story before writing it down, or use their bodies to form geometric shapes or demonstrate the movement of planets. I watched Michael, a second grader with language-processing problems, working on an alphabet book. The book was to include an action word for each letter of the alphabet. As Michael thought of each word, he would break from his seat and move his body to act out the word he was about to write. When he came to the letter "m," he hunched over, curled his arms under, and did a bouncy monkey walk for a moment. He then

*In personal Math Puzzles books, students use words
and drawings to show multiplication problems.*

popped back into his chair and started writing "monkey." I helped him convert the noun to a verb phrase, "monkeying around."

Later, in a sharing circle, Michael stood up and led his peers in a short conversation about the letter "m": "In my alphabet book, I wrote an action word for 'm'—monkeying around. Do you have another different word for 'm'?" A couple of children raised their hands and offered other "m" action words. Michael's willingness to take the risk of teaching his peers came, I think, from the confidence he gathered from acting out his words and then slowly spelling them into his alphabet book. He was sure in his mind and his body that he was right.

The examples and suggestions in this book illustrate how to integrate the arts into lessons in as many forms as possible. The goal is that each child will find a favorite option at least once during the day, and over time, all students will have the opportunity to lead with their strengths. By integrating the arts, we allow children to play on all their strings.

Reason 2:
The Arts Encourage
Joyful, Active Learning

Every Saturday, the grandchildren come to my house to play. Sylvie usually asks, "What are we going to do today, Bubbe?" And I respond with a list of choices: "We can draw or paint; we can read a book; we can play cards or dominoes or catch; we can do a puzzle; we can dress up and have a tea party …." The list is a long one, everything on it is full of learning and fun, and everything on it is attractive to the children.

Why should school be any less engaging? Why not appeal to children's innate yearning for fun? I watched Richard Lewis, director of the Touchstone Center for the Arts in New York City, captivate a kindergarten class by walking into their classroom when they were studying the ocean, taking off his shoes, rolling up his pants, and tiptoeing across the floor. "Why are you walking like that?" the children asked. "So I don't get my pants wet in the ocean," he said. They stepped into his drama. "Watch out for that shark!" they warned, and Richard leaped and dodged. At age five, the trip from here to anywhere is a short one, and a piece of theater like that has instant results. The children were ready now to think and write about the ocean with new excitement and curiosity.

The fact that students are having fun and being playful is not a sign that work has stopped. On the contrary, the real work of a fully-engaged brain—gathering new data and connecting it with old—may be just beginning. "Play is children's work," Piaget tells us. If work is defined as exertion directed to producing or accomplishing something, then many types of productive play are important educational work.

Theater games provide a way to study history, current events, literature, and even the systems of the body or the process of photosynthesis. Hopscotch is both fun and educational if the squares are marked with spelling or vocabulary or Spanish words. Children almost always enjoy making images, and those images can demonstrate their understanding of a character in a novel or the geographic landscape of a region. The dress-up corner can spark narrative writing. An explanation of the steps of a line dance can develop into expository writing. When we use the arts to get the work of the curriculum done, we soften the hard line that is so often drawn between play and work and increase the possibility of joyful learning.

The power of surprise

One of the reasons that working with the arts is fun is that the work is full of surprises. For example, writing poetry tips you into a new place. You have to think in pictures. You have to talk in a condensed language. You have to tell the truth or the poem sounds lame, even to you, or especially to you.

One of my favorite moments in school is when a visiting poet begins to read to the children. Michael Dennis Browne, a poet and teacher in Minneapolis, entrances whole-school audiences through gentle surprises. Here's a poem written by his young son, Peter McLean-Browne.

My Rat

His eyes are like shimmering rubies on a necklace of light.
His hair is like sunrays woven into his body.
His voice is as soft as a bed made out of rainbow-colored silk.
His feet are as swift as the wind.
His voice is as dark and gruff as a storm raging in us filling with darkness.
His tail is as weak as a fish out of water, but as long as the patience of someone always waiting forever and ever.
His teeth are as shiny as the bright jewel in the center of the earth.
When he cries he makes a flood of clearness.
He is crying right now, because it's the end of this poem.

After three or four such poems, the air changes. Children listen with more edge. They wait for the surprise. They expect the unexpected. As the oddness of poetry sucks them in, they begin to develop agile minds.

Reason 3: The Arts Help Students Make and Express Personal Connections to Content

It is a truism (with a lot of research behind it) that children are reluctant to learn something in which they have little interest. Researcher Geoffrey Caine says, "We need to help learners create a felt meaning, a sense of relationship with a subject, in addition to an intellectual understanding." (D'Arcangelo 1998, 24) Relevance, a connection to life outside of school or to other things they've already experienced and learned, helps children care about what is newly presented to them and to make meaning from it. For most children, the arts provide a natural route for connecting with the curriculum in a personally meaningful way.

Fifth grade students in Minneapolis study ecosystems and are required to learn a basic vocabulary related to environmental studies. Teacher Erin Klug and artist Usry Alleyne helped students use poetry, drawing, and videography to make and express a personal connection to the topic. They invited students to study and describe an environment they personally enjoyed, using the vocabulary words that they'd learned: "environment," "tolerate," "prefer," "organism," and the names of the five senses. Many chose their own rooms, drawing pictures and writing poetry to describe the space—and the lives that filled that space.

They then videotaped the images, reading their poetry off-camera. The children edited and polished their writing. They practiced reading smoothly and with expression. The project not only absorbed the students, but their focus and effort paid off in work they could share with pride and in a new understanding about what really makes a viable environment.

When I wanted to teach a group of children about the material simplicity of tribal people's lives, I showed the children a picture drawn by an Inuit hunter of all the things he owned, titled *Things in My Life*. There were about twenty objects on the page. I then asked the children to draw a picture of the things in their lives and gave them a large piece of white paper. The children filled the papers. Many resorted to lists of words and finally gave up on that, too. In the discussion that followed we heard, "Look at all that stuff I have and he has only a few things to take care of." "How did they do it? How did they get along with so little?" Not only did the children learn about an important aspect of Inuit life, but they also challenged their assumptions about what's necessary to live a life.

Self-expression

One of the most important payoffs of using the arts as a teaching tool is the many opportunities they provide for a diverse group of children to express their thoughts and feelings, and in the process to share something vital about who they are. In the midst of the homogeneity of the school curriculum, the opportunity to sing your own song is a gift.

In arts residencies designed by my daughter, teacher and artist Elizabeth Crawford, we used the arts to help children understand issues of exclusion, discrimination, and cliques. We asked the children to write poetry about their feelings when they or someone they cared about was excluded or included in a game, a party, or just in conversations. Then they made large drawings of themselves at a time of exclusion or inclusion. The bodies expressed sadness or happiness in both the faces and figures. These drawings were mounted on corrugated cardboard and then placed around the school in settings that seemed natural to the figure (on the playground, in the lunch room, etc.) After photographing the figures in their settings, we exhibited the slides (with a projector) and the figures (standing around as a set) during a performance of the children reciting their poetry. The cumulative effect of the drawings, the slides, and the poetry powerfully evoked the hurt and happiness we cause one another by rejection and acceptance. This was a rather elaborate project, but the poems or the figures alone would have provided an effective reminder of the costs of exclusive behavior. Our goal in such arts-inclusive activities is to make an environment in which personal expression is safe and valued.

Reason 4:
The Arts Help Children Understand and Express Abstract Concepts

Science writer Patricia Wolfe says, "Many of our strongest neural networks are formed by actual experience. Without the concrete experience [of a subject], the representation or symbol may have little meaning, no matter how much someone explains it to you." (Wolfe 2001, 137–8) Storytelling and movement help Peter Lawton's first grade students at City of Lakes Waldorf School in Minneapolis learn beginning math concepts. The children hear stories and recite poems that have numbers buried in them, stories about Sister Hazel, who walks with even steps; Uncle Albert, who walks with a cane and heavily on every other step; Junior, who runs and kicks up his heels on every third step; and the giant Finn M'Coul, whose mighty strides cover ten steps! As they recite, they move in a circle, emphasizing the number sets—of ones, twos, threes, up to tens—about which they are chanting. The recitations and movement provide physical and imaginative access to the abstractions of addition and multiplication.

During social studies, simulated interviews, role plays, and reenactments can help bring a period of history to life. For example, in a unit on westward expansion in the nineteenth century, two students might simulate a conversation between two children traveling in a covered wagon. Likewise, movement and drawing can help clarify scientific processes and poetry's concrete images can help express big ideas. Effective learning moves from the known to the unknown, from the familiar and personal to abstract understandings. The arts help students to make these leaps with confidence.

Reason 5:
The Arts Stimulate
Higher-Level Thinking

There are basically three kinds of thinking that we want to encourage in our children: attending, discerning, and inventing. Attending and discerning are the more analytical skills. They involve paying attention, reporting accurately, sifting through information, and noticing the relationships among the facts explored. Inventing takes students one step further to building upon what they have previously learned and thought so they can make new meaning (for example, solving a problem or creating a new approach or vision). It requires an imaginative understanding.

A fourth/fifth grade class at Prairie Creek Community School in Northfield, Minnesota, wanted to challenge the whole school to think deeply about hunger and the distribution of the world's food supply. Using colored tape, the class outlined a rough map of the world on the floor of the gym. Then during a whole school assembly, they told a story about people from different countries each getting different amounts of food. That seemed pretty obvious to the children—different numbers of people need different amounts to feed their numbers.

As the students narrated, however, people were selected to dramatize the story. Each country was allotted the number of people that represented their percentage of the world's population and the amount of food represented by that country's actual share of the world's food. When most of the school had crowded into China and were given a tiny bag of candies while a handful of people in the USA were given a large bucket of candy, the children were amazed and incensed. Even the class that had researched the topic seemed impressed by the dramatized reality of the distribution. In a discussion afterwards, these five- to eleven-year-olds struggled to come up with new solutions for the world's food distribution problems. Throughout the project the children attended to new information, discerned inequities, and invented/imagined new ways to do things.

The task of developing children's capacity to do all three kinds of thinking cries for the interjection of the arts. The arts provide the tools to help students develop the intellectual muscle for paying careful attention, recording accurately, and analyzing from multiple points of view. And they offer one of the few reliable routes to understanding the world not only as it is, but as we might imagine it to be. The arts will help our students develop minds spry and courageous enough to function at a high level in a world constantly in flux.

Reason 6:
The Arts Build Community and Help Children Develop Collaborative Work Skills

As visiting teachers in an arts residency focused on multicultural understanding, my daughter Elizabeth and I were using storytelling, poetry, music, dance, and visual art to help the children in a small K–5 elementary school appreciate a culture very different from any they had ever known—that of the Inuit of the Canadian Arctic. At the end of our weeks together, everyone assembled in a huge circle in the gym. We had come to enjoy Arctic games—playful, competitive demonstrations of skills such as blindfold balance-beam walking, arm pulls, and relay races.

The final game event was the high kick. A helper held a stick that had a small piece of bone dangling from the end by a cord. The bone was at a low level, easy to kick. The player ran towards it, and leaping from one foot, tried to kick the piece of bone. The helper then held the stick a little higher and then higher, and the trick was to see how high each player could kick.

After each kicker went as high as he or she thought possible, I invited the whole group in the outer circle to help in the way the Inuit do. We chanted together, "Aiaiaiaiaiai . . .," as the kicker ran towards the bone, and then "yah!" as the kicker leaped in the air. Without fail, with the chant in their ears, the kickers went far higher in their leaps than they or the audience had thought they could. The point of the lesson was that a crucial element in the survival of the Inuit for thousands of years, in one of the earth's least hospitable environments, has been their understanding that the united effort of the group makes possible what no individual can do alone.

Educators have always known, and research is now confirming, that children's deepest, longest-lasting learning comes when they are working with others. Teachers at every level understand the value of having students work in small groups to solve problems and demonstrate their understanding. Peers serve as "highly available and active companions, providing each other with motivation, imagination, and opportunities for creative elaboration of the activities of their community." (Rogoff 1990, ix)

Doing creative things together creates and sustains community. It also promotes the type of learning that is retained long after a project is complete and that motivates future exploration. Children working together on a piece of art will engage in intense social interaction, absorb and expand their learning, and perhaps lift the project to a level of imaginative expression and understanding that one student alone could not manage.

In a collaborative mural project, for example, students must pay careful attention to each other's work to ensure that the images ultimately connect to make a single, group-generated image. In a mural project sponsored by Origins, teacher-artist Elizabeth Crawford directed the construction of a large clay mural in which separately constructed tiles ultimately fit together like a huge puzzle. Collaboration was required in every step of the process.

First, children came up with ideas for images to illustrate a theme from their curriculum. Everyone created at least one image in a pencil drawing. Next, they worked out a design for the mural using all the drawings, transferred the mural design to a large template, and laid a grid over the template.

Each child translated the drawing from one square of the grid into clay, making certain to match lines and shapes with contiguous squares. The children knew that their individual pieces contributed to the quality of the whole composition and most stayed focused and careful. After the teacher fired the clay squares, the children painted them and assembled them into a complete picture that was mortared to the wall. A collaborative *tour de force!*

Music, too, provides wonderful opportunities for collaboration with harmonies, rounds, and call-and-response songs and chants. Ghanaian musician Sowah Mensah taught a group of students to drum in the manner of indigenous African ensemble playing, with its complex interweaving rhythms. In this form of musical collaboration, drummers make music as both separate *and* connected players. When Sowah taught this form of ensemble playing to eighth grade students, they learned about a culture in which tension between the individual and the group is desirable and natural—indeed, the source of good music. And in learning this, they learned a valuable lesson in the skills and benefits of collaboration.

Even poetry, a solitary art, finds a form of collaboration in class poems written with the teacher as scribe, or in literary magazines organized around themes, or just collected and edited by the children as the annual literary publication. Child editors work with child writers. Student graphic

The final step in creating this ceramic mural was to combine individually-made tiles into one fluid, complete image.

designers work together, cutting and pasting. The result is distributed in the school and to parents, and a poetry reading crowns the collective effort. In all these examples, children learn collaboration by practicing it in arts-integrated projects that they love. And through continued practice of collaboration, they deepen their sense of connection to each other.

The Friend of Learning

In the book *What Is Art For?*, scholar Ellen Dissanayake suggests that when we apply art to a task we elaborate upon the task, putting our mark upon it in such a way that it is more special and therefore more meaningful to us and to others. [Dissanayake 1988, 92] The maker is connected in a more intimate way to what he has made, to the world, and to the people who see and use the artful thing. The maker thereby becomes more able, lively, confident, and connected. When we make our marks, we establish a place in the world for ourselves.

In this book, there are many examples of children who have been given the opportunity to make their marks, to elaborate, to make special. Some of the examples may strike the reader as true art, others as more making than art-making. I have not been very concerned to restrain my examples to "pure" art experiences, whatever those are, but rather to give as many instances as possible of children elaborating upon the curriculum until they make it special and thereby their own. And when they do, they begin to love learning.

Works Cited

D'Arcangelo, Marcia. 1998. "The Brains Behind the Brain." ASCD *Educational Leadership*. (November): 20–26.

Dissanayake, Ellen. 1988. *What is Art For?* Seattle: University of Washington Press.

Rogoff, Barbara. 1990. *Apprenticeship in Thinking: Cognitive Development in Social Context.* New York: Oxford University Press USA.

Wolfe, Patricia. 2001. *Brain Matters: Translating Research into Classroom Practice.* Alexandria, VA: Association for Supervision and Curriculum Development (ASCD).

CHAPTER 2

Creating a Safe Environment for Arts-Integration

A fourth grade teacher friend noted that when she attempted her annual collaborative mural project in September instead of the usual January, students didn't have the necessary work skills and social skills to do a good job. Indeed, rushing to build models or paint or act out the movement of food along the human digestive track can result in the frequently heard teacher comment, "I don't do art projects with my kids. They can't handle it." But perhaps with attention paid to creating a safe environment, they can.

In this chapter, I'll present steps that teachers can take to help create a safe, friendly environment for working with the arts:

• Establish clear rules and expectations for children's behavior.

• Provide a structure for collaborative work.

• Pay attention to how you respond to creative work.

• Provide a physical environment that nurtures creative work.

Establish Clear Rules and Expectations for Children's Behavior

I recently attended a sixth graders' meeting in which there was a lot of student participation that generated some good ideas. However, the students continually interrupted each other and the teacher; there were put-downs and side conversations; and some students sat silently throughout the meeting. The conversation seemed always on the edge of falling apart with an adult repeatedly pulling it back from the brink of chaos. What was missing were established, accepted classroom rules and habits that could guide the students in their work together.

Before introducing arts projects, particularly projects involving collaborative work, it's important to be clear about rules and expectations. Think and talk with the children about the following questions:

- How should we treat each other when we work together?

- How should we speak to each other?

- How should we take care of our space and our materials?

- How should we behave when we're engaged in movement or theater activities?

Model and practice desired behaviors

Once the rules are established, you'll want to spend time modeling and practicing how the rules apply to specific situations. For example, students will need to see and then practice how to move safely during theater or movement activities. The text box on the next page outlines the steps in a careful modeling process, and throughout the book you'll find examples of modeling the specific behaviors needed for success with particular projects.

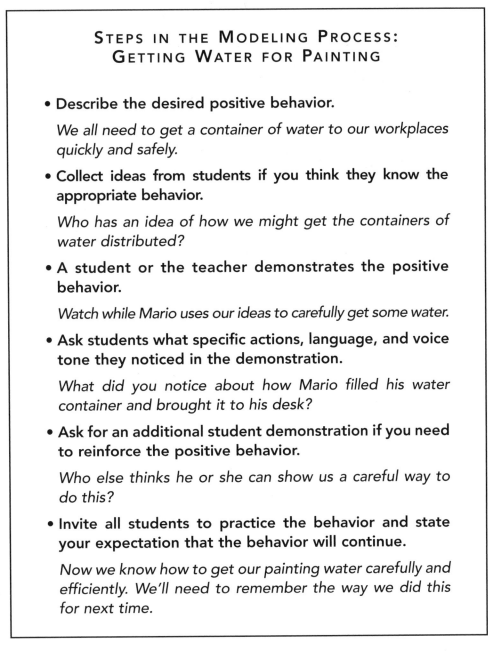

STEPS IN THE MODELING PROCESS: GETTING WATER FOR PAINTING

- **Describe the desired positive behavior.**

  We all need to get a container of water to our workplaces quickly and safely.

- **Collect ideas from students if you think they know the appropriate behavior.**

  Who has an idea of how we might get the containers of water distributed?

- **A student or the teacher demonstrates the positive behavior.**

  Watch while Mario uses our ideas to carefully get some water.

- **Ask students what specific actions, language, and voice tone they noticed in the demonstration.**

  What did you notice about how Mario filled his water container and brought it to his desk?

- **Ask for an additional student demonstration if you need to reinforce the positive behavior.**

  Who else thinks he or she can show us a careful way to do this?

- **Invite all students to practice the behavior and state your expectation that the behavior will continue.**

  Now we know how to get our painting water carefully and efficiently. We'll need to remember the way we did this for next time.

Have a process in place
for responding to rule breaking

But what happens when children don't follow the rules? It's bound to happen, particularly when you're first working with arts activities. So, once you've established the rules, think about, discuss, model, and practice what will happen when children don't follow the rules. Children need direct, calm reminders that they have broken a rule. They need the opportunity to center themselves and bring themselves back to a condition where they can behave in ways that support the group.

One common response when a child is beginning to lose self-control is to ask the child to briefly leave the group:

> *Carlos, take a break.*

> *Jessica, regroup please.*

> *Candace, you need a vacation.*

The goal of "taking a break" isn't punishment. Instead, it is designed to give children the chance, while they are still mostly in control of themselves, to pull back to their best, most cooperative selves.

Establish a signal for quiet

Visual and auditory signals such as a raised hand or a rhythmic clap are quick, reliable ways to get children's silent attention. Whatever signal you use, it needs to be simple and easily seen or heard. Once you've introduced and modeled the signal, and the children have practiced responding, it's important to use it consistently whenever you want silent attention (for example, in the middle of a work period or when gathering the children for a work sharing circle). It is also very important to model and practice the signal again whenever attention to it starts to slip (which inevitably it will!) in order to keep the signal effective all year long.

Provide a Structure for Collaborative Work

It's an excellent idea to include the arts in the first collaborative projects you do. The workers, usually eager to do the work, persevere to completion because of their intense interest in both the product and the process. Any teacher who has helped children produce a play, for example, knows the infectious excitement that permeates the whole process, even if the "play" is no more than a small group of first graders practicing for ten minutes so that they can retell a story in mime. They manage through all the chatter and silliness to pull the "show" together:

"Carmen! We need Carmen to be Martha. Go get her."

"I'll be George."

"What'll I do? I don't have a part."

"You can be the narrator. You're a good reader. You read the story and we'll move."

"OK. Carmen's here."

The narrator begins reading.

But successful collaboration doesn't happen automatically. The teacher needs to provide structure and give children many opportunities to practice. It's a spiral process in which every step towards self-control means that children are able to handle more active collaboration and that collaboration, in turn, builds greater self-control. Here are some ideas for making collaboration successful:

Model and practice

With a small group of children, model for the class an example of a high-functioning work group. Then let them discuss what they noticed about the group's behavior. Give everyone a chance to practice with quick, easy assignments before they tackle longer, harder ones.

Vary groupings

Make sure that everyone gets a chance to work with everyone else. Watch for good combinations so you can repeat them at times.

Orchestrate

Schedule frequent check-ins with the groups. Talk children through the steps at first, so everyone is successful. Check in often as to the status of the groups, then less often as collaboration skills develop.

Problem-solve sticky situations

Role-play various group work scenarios. Brainstorm together what to say and do in the sticky situations. Teach techniques that equalize participation, such as distributing tokens for opportunities to talk.

Pay Attention to How You Respond to Creative Work

Sharing work-in-progress as well as the finished product is an important part of working in an art form. But in order for sharing to be a positive experience, it is important to teach, model, and practice how to make respectful, helpful, caring responses. In Chapter 10 you'll find information on helping students learn to respond effectively to each other's work.

But it's also important to think about your own responses. How you respond to students' work moment after moment, day after day is central to what children learn about how to respond to each other. Throughout the book you'll see examples of teacher responses, often set off in italics.

Phoebe, this drawing is really fun to look at. I can see that you were showing people with all different types of hair—straight and curly and wavy, short and long. Let's see…which kind of hair do I have?

You just made a prediction, Mohammed, and I'll bet it will turn out that you're right—this man is a gentle person.

I like your character, DeVon. He's funny! What does he look like?

The red and green in this picture really jump out.

Instead of offering general praise, these comments are specific, interested, and personal, based on close attention and noticing.

Work then pause to notice. Work then pause to notice. That's the rhythm of a classroom environment that encourages ideas. We are all showing our work to each other and we are all paying attention to that work.

Provide a Physical Environment that Nurtures Creative Work

An environment that nurtures creative work is one in which space, time, materials, and equipment all support the integration of the arts into everyday teaching. Following are some ideas for working within existing resources to create a physical environment that welcomes the arts.

Pay attention to how you use space

To make it possible for children to learn through movement and rhythms, especially those children whose learning strength is kinesthetic and/or musical, the classroom needs to have some open space. At the least, furniture arrangement needs to be flexible enough to permit quick rearrangement. If you want to invite children to express creatively the structure of a molecule or the hibernation of a bear, for example, adequate space will make it much easier for them to do so.

Open space also makes improvisational dramatic retellings more likely. It makes possible larger-scale visual work when a student is so inclined. And perhaps most important of all, it makes it more convenient and therefore more likely that students will circle up to listen to each other tell stories, make music, or read poetry, or to look at each other's visual art.

The classroom environment can also communicate that exciting sense of "your work is what matters most here" by the way its walls are used. Displays of student work demonstrate to students and to visitors that what is important here is what we generate from our own minds and with our own hands. So, let the walls show the children's thoughts, their work-in-progress, and their finished products.

Pay attention to how you use time

The rush to fit everything required of teachers and students into a school day—the curriculum, the tests, the standards, eating, exercise, fresh air, and the many transitions in between all these—makes lack of time the most often heard complaint in schools. And often the schedule dictates that what little time there is be carved into many small pieces. There is no time for sustained thought; learning is chopped up into disconnected, topic-specific units; and fast results are valued over depth of understanding

In museums, I watch many children, especially very young ones, fix on an experiential exhibit. They operate the machine or move through the steps over and over. Parents, on the other hand, often urge the children to move on: "There are so many more exhibits to see. Look over there—

*A paper quilt made of illustrated reports about
animals hangs on a hallway display board.*

that one looks great." In the effort to ensure that the child doesn't miss anything good, and sometimes in the restlessness of an adult temperament, no investigation is sustained to a level where the child can begin to make connections with what she already knows and thus begin forging an idea new to her.

Valuing the chance for extended work in the classroom means prioritizing longer stretches of time whenever possible. It helps, of course, if extended periods of work time are valued by the teaching and administrative staff as a whole. A schedule designed around the vision of children having enough time to reflect is a schedule likely to result in more imaginative thinking. Time to mess around, to play out the whole rope of our interest, pays off in original thinking.

Choose arts-friendly materials

Bringing the arts into the classroom does not require purchasing expensive materials. It does, however, require paying attention to the materials you have and providing a wide range of simple materials. For example, some drawing materials are more flexible and provide more options than others. Markers are good for posters or writing on a chart. They add dynamism and fun. But they do not blend well and cannot be mixed to create new colors. It's not easy to vary intensity with markers either, so they are not very useful for showing the nuances required in accurate or expressive details.

Along with markers, provide crayons, colored pencils, pastels, or paint. If a child is doing an observational drawing of a plant or bird or even a rock, she can use crayon or colored pencil colors laid one on top of another to create a color that more nearly matches the subject. A child can also use

pencils to show shading and nuance. You can graduate a red pencil, shading off to lighter and lighter red, and finally blending to buff to distinguish a female cardinal from the solid red of the male cardinal.

The right furniture and equipment can spark the young inventor, too. A drama center that is flexible can transform into a huge variety of settings. You can make the drama space fairly elaborate or keep to the essentials—some space, a table, chairs, and perhaps a shelf. Invention can do the rest. Simple materials that can be used creatively will help. Pieces of cloth in different textures, colors, and sizes can be turned into clothing, scenery, flags, tablecloths, and swimming pools. A box of long things, round things, square things—a variety of shapes—inspires props for a wide range of scenarios.

At any grade level, actors, directors, set-designers, and prop users will improvise simulations from history or literature if given adaptable materials, an appropriate structure, and the opportunity to invent. You'll find examples of using theater in the classroom in Chapter 6, "Getting Comfortable with Theater," and in many of the subject-specific chapters.

When choosing materials, it's also important to think about what images you'll have available, on the wall or in folders, to spark writing ideas. The image of a person looking confused or excited, or friends with their arms around each other, will offer an open-ended invitation to writing in a variety of genres: dialogue, poetry, a story, or even an essay. The idea, as with the furnishings and props, is to have the images be suggestive but not explicit, so that there is mental space to choose and invent. Landscapes are good for this. Old calendars provide an inexpensive variety of exciting settings in which to place characters and then make up what happens to them in that place.

FLEXIBLE ART SUPPLIES

(Items can be stored in trays or boxes, each in its own clearly labeled container.)

- Assorted papers in varied sizes —newsprint, manila, colored construction paper, watercolor paper, white painting paper, rolls of mural paper, colored tissue paper, white bond/copy paper

- Pencils—#2 and either #2B or 4B (for a darker, softer tone)

- Charcoal pencils

- Erasers—white or pink pearl work well

- Pens—cheap ballpoint pens and ink flow pens such as Sharpies or Pilot drawing pens

- Crayons, oil pastels, colored chalks, colored pencils, markers

- Tempera paint—gel or liquid

- Watercolor paint

- Brushes in varied sizes—#12 natural bristle, flat and round, are good basic brushes

- Containers for water—coffee cans or reused plastic containers

- Plastic plates—these make great reusable paint palettes, particularly the three-part divided plates

- Sponges, paper towels

- Scissors

- Masking and transparent tape

- Stapler and staples

- White glue and paste

- Wet clay in an airtight container; newspapers; tongue depressors and old pencils for carving and texturing clay

- Plasticene

- Rubber bands

- Sandpaper

- Florist's wire and pipe cleaners

- Yarn and string

- Felt

- Recycled and natural materials —acorns, bark, beads, bottle caps, buttons, cardboard, corks, cotton balls, feathers, foil, magazines, paper bags, pebbles, pinecones, spools, toothpicks, wood scraps, paper and fabric scraps for collages (wallpaper, wrapping paper, etc.)

- Interesting objects to handle, including natural objects such as shells and rocks

- Smocks—old shirts or aprons

- Storage space for children's folders

- Pictures/postcards/slides of art from around the world

- Books

Provide equipment whose use is open-ended

The environment for inventiveness might also include equipment that is open-ended. Blocks are an open-ended material that invite the making of something from scratch: replicas of buildings observed; settings for stories; models of places visited in field trips; designs for a new school or library or bedroom. A whole curriculum can revolve around students using three-dimensional building models to show what they've learned. Blocks are a generic tool for learning about the world by recreating it either as you see it or as you wish it to be.

A sand table can also have multiple uses, particularly if you install one that can convert into a water table, complete with a small motor to create flow. Then you are off to the invention of meandering rivers, falls, eddies, and dams. These can provide the setting for simulations of nature's way with water and sand. Young inventors can test hypotheses or even create three-dimensional models of geographic locations they have seen or read about in fiction or nonfiction. One fifth grade teacher put out the water table each year for the unit on landforms—it was the center for conjecturing about and exploring the relationship between earth and water.

Easy access to open-ended materials and equipment is a constant invitation to do interesting and meaningful work. The catch is that those things must be kept in good order and condition. If they are abused, they will dry up or break down and be useless. If they are not neatly arranged and labeled, if they are not taken out and put away carefully with each use, they will soon be inaccessible. So take the time to teach how to use and care for materials, encouraging children to practice use and care before actually using any materials.

*A calendar picture prompts a second grader to write a story
about a beautiful place that she visited with her father and brother.*

Getting Comfortable with Using the Arts

After establishing the basics for a classroom environment that supports arts-integration, the next step is for you and the students to feel more comfortable working with individual art forms.

Often when I ask teachers if they use drawing (or singing, or movement, or theater) in their teaching, the fast and definitive answer is, "I can't draw [sing, dance, tell stories….]." In response, I ask them to consider converting "I can't" to a statement of possibility:

"I'm *learning* to draw."

"I'm *learning* to sing."

"I'm *learning* to tell stories."

Such declarations will express to your students that you are a learner right along with them, that they too can learn to draw or sing or write poetry, that learning a skill is a process that takes time and practice, a matter of evolving know-how. When their teacher walks into new and scary territory to stretch her skills, children who secretly believe that they cannot read or write a story or do multiplication may gather their courage and go for it.

In the next five chapters, I present some of the fundamental skills involved in drawing, music, movement, theater, and poetry and I give suggestions about how to practice these skills with your students until you all have a degree of comfort and confidence. Here are a few general guidelines:

1. Start slowly.

At first, focus on one or two art forms. Pick ones that seem more familiar and comfortable because of your past experience with them.

2. Learn and teach some basic skills in the art form itself before integrating it into curriculum content.

When learning basic skills, start with techniques that feel safe and easy, and then slowly stretch the boundaries.

3. Learn with the children.

Although it's a good idea to try out each skill-building technique yourself before teaching it to the children, you don't need to get good at it first. Your risk-taking will inspire them in more than just the arts.

4. Turn to other teachers and adult community members for advice, training, encouragement, ideas, etc.

If you are lucky enough to have an art or music teacher on your staff, let that teacher know that you are hoping to give your students additional drawing or casual singing experiences. Talk about your goals; ask for support and partnership. There will surely be times and places where the work you are each doing can be integrated. Use contact with other adults, too, and books, exhibits, and performances you attend, to stretch your appreciation, skills, and willingness to take risks. Above all, use your exploration into the arts to bring you the pleasure of self-expression, beauty, and authenticity. You and the students deserve nothing less!

Getting Comfortable with Drawing

Visual representation is one of the most convenient and effective tools for teaching all subjects in the academic curriculum. Making papier-mâché or clay models, collaborating on a mural, drawing a map, and creating cardboard cutouts all help bring the curriculum alive and make content accessible for those who learn best by seeing and doing rather than hearing. Throughout the book, I offer examples of using various visual arts media to learn and to share learning.

In this chapter, however, I focus on drawing because if students are going to use drawing effectively, they first need to learn basic skills. Once students gain some basic drawing skills, they can use drawing frequently and effectively to accurately represent their perceptions of literature, plants and animals, machines, or events in history. They will have a new ability to make "sananguac," the Inuit word for "a little reality." But if students can't draw with some level of accuracy then they cannot rigorously demonstrate what they are learning. Rough approximations and generic figures and objects will not show what they know. Accurate drawing will allow two payoffs: the children can use their visual strengths to learn, and you can use their drawings to assess that learning.

Learning to Draw

In *Drawing on the Right Side of the Brain,* Betty Edwards says that when people say they don't know how to draw, the real problem is that they don't know how to see. (Edwards 1989) Learning to draw is actually a process of sharpening the capacity to see what is out there and then responding to what we see by making marks on paper.

Artists have a large stock of images in their visual memories. But most of us cannot call up an accurate picture of something we wish to draw, so we make it up, guessing at shapes and lines.

When we try to draw a dog or a car, we may get stuck early on and be disappointed in the results because we are trying to draw what the subject looks like, but have no mental picture to follow.

Observational drawing is a good place to begin learning to draw because you draw while you are observing a subject. In observational drawing, you need to open your eyes, look hard, and drop preconceptions about what you think you're going to see.

In this chapter, I present quick lessons that will help develop observational drawing skills. It's a good idea for teachers to try these exercises themselves before presenting them to the children. Once you've tried a drawing yourself, it will be easier to model the step-by-step process for the children. But this doesn't mean that you need to become a proficient artist before introducing drawing to the children. When you feel that you understand the sequence of the lesson and have a plan for presenting that sequence to your students, you're ready to go.

Don't apologize for your lack of artistic skill. You will only model such apology-making for the children. Confidence develops with practice. As you and the children make drawing after drawing, slowly you all become better at drawing. And as you apply yourselves systematically to this task, as with just about any consistent practice in an art form, you become better learners.

Finding the time for drawing exercises

"OK," you might say, "I'm willing to give this a try. But how will I fit drawing lessons into my already overloaded day?" Transitions and the little pieces of time left over from other lessons are useful for brief drawing lessons:

> We have ten minutes before lunch—a little time to draw! Please put away your math books, but keep your pencils out. On this paper I am handing out, draw some geometric shapes. The ones we have been studying may come to mind, and you can look around the classroom to see shapes everywhere. Just make simple outline drawings. When you have four or five drawings, you can elaborate on them—add texture or some dark and light tones to make the shapes stand out.

A drawing exercise can calm and center children when they are too unfocused to jump right into a formal lesson. It can provide a few quiet minutes at the end of the day, before lunch or a closing activity, or as a settling down after a transition. For example, I have used drawing exercises after recess to focus the children and help them segue back into academics.

Observational Drawing Lessons

(Illustrations by Elizabeth Crawford)

Warm-ups

Warm-up drawing exercises can help develop basic coordination and observation skills. They are ideal at the beginning of the day, during a quiet time after lunch, or to sharpen focus before a lesson.

Circles and squares

As a pre-warm-up to the warm-up, make rapid large, looping lines; sharp straight lines; scribbled circles and squares of different sizes. After a minute of this, hands and fingers are literally warmed up and better coordinated. Then draw a series of circles and squares, trying for evenness of the shapes. Try moving your hand and positioning it in different ways (lifting your wrist off the table, using your whole arm, pushing lines away from you versus pulling them toward you, etc.); notice whether you have different control and different results. Generally speaking, try to maintain a loose movement and avoid stiffening or locking your hand, wrist, or arm against the drawing surface. This exercise creates greater dexterity and teaches the importance of positioning and movement.

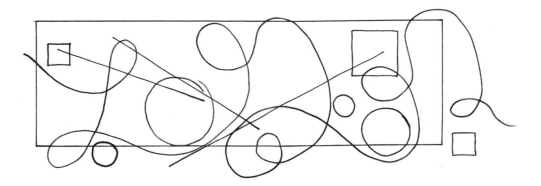

Looking for shapes and lines

Try to find familiar, simple shapes and lines in the objects in the classroom. You will see many circles, squares, polygons of all shapes, and curving and straight lines in the parts and pieces of more complex forms. Draw those shapes or parts of the shapes on a piece of paper. At the end, a few people might each show a shape or line, and the group can guess where that shape is in the classroom. Of course, it will probably be in more places than one, but looking for it will help students to start carefully noticing lines and shapes. This can be a quick prelude to a drawing activity or to a scientific observation or even a lesson on using descriptive language.

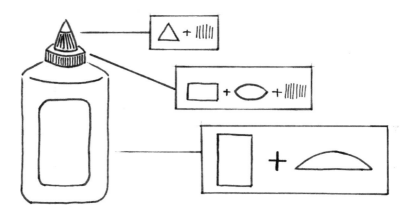

Mirror reflection

Draw a vertical line down the middle of a piece of paper. On one half of the paper, draw a shape, using a single line that begins and ends against the straight vertical line. Now draw a "reflection" of the shape on the other side of the line. The first time you try this, you can make the initial "half drawing" ahead of time, if you wish, and photocopy it for everyone to work on.

Memory exercises

Look at a simple drawing for twenty to sixty seconds, depending on skill level, then try to duplicate the drawing without looking at it. Start with a non-realistic drawing composed of a few lines and shapes. Then work up to more complex compositions, including realistic images of animals, people, or objects. Here is one to start with.

Talking through a drawing

This may well become your most frequently used method for increasing observational drawing skills. Choose a simple two-dimensional drawing of an animal or plant or object. You may need to create a large copy of it for easier viewing. Thoroughly describe and discuss the visual features of the drawing. Identify the shapes and connections between the shapes, the relative sizes of the parts that make up the overall forms, etc. For example, if you and the students are looking at a drawing

of a bird, students might notice the oval-shaped body, the round head and round eye, the triangle shapes of its crest and beak. You could ask them to compare the size of the crest and the beak and to notice where the round shape of the eye is located within the round shape of the head.

After you've looked for shapes, begin the drawing, breaking down the image into simple parts so that you and the students can see them and see how to put them together to create a likeness of the subject. Have a large blank sheet of paper ready for you to draw the various components of the bird in front of the class, and make sure that students also have a blank sheet of paper ready so they can draw along with you. Start by identifying together a large, central shape in the subject (the shape of the bird's body, for example), then draw it on your sheet. You can ask students for help in deciding where on the page it should go. Remind students that you'll need room in all directions for the rest of the drawing. Then ask them to put that same shape in approximately the same place on their papers.

Next, you and the students identify and draw a line or shape that is next to or inside of the starting shape. Continue in this fashion—moving out from the original shape, connecting shape to shape, line to line, until you and the students have drawn all the shapes and lines in the image. It can help to name the shapes: "The bird's crest looks like jagged mountain peaks." "The clown's head and hat make an upside-down ice cream cone." Here is a drawing you can try and then teach, with a guide for the sequence of shapes and lines:

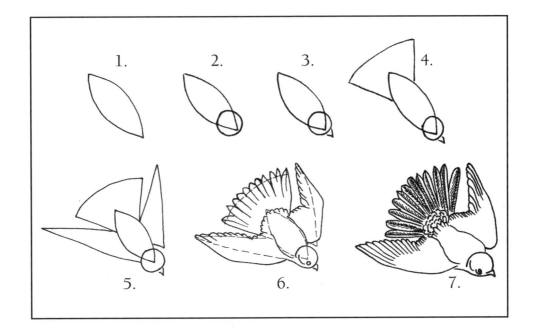

If something looks odd, draw a correcting line or shape right over it. If when you're done the whole thing looks wrong to you, try it again if you have time, or talk with the children about what seems off and how you might change that when you draw a bird again.

Once you and the children feel some confidence with replicating drawn, two-dimensional images, you can move on to photographs and then simple three-dimensional objects.

Tracing through a window and copying

Place pieces of tracing paper over a window facing the outside. Trace what you see through the window, without changing your position, so that the object or scene before you remains constant. Then draw a copy of the tracing on a piece of paper, trying to maintain accuracy of perspective and detail. This increases observation skills and illustrates the phenomenon of perspective, because in the tracing, the more distant objects will automatically be smaller than those up front.

Drawing upside down

Choose a drawing composed of lines only (no lights and darks). Turn the image upside down and copy it. This helps you and the students actually see the lines as lines, instead of putting lines down as you think they should be. To test this phenomenon you can copy the image right side up as well and compare the accuracy of the two drawings.

Drawing with volume

In order to have a drawn object look less flat and more like three-dimensional reality, you need to add the illusion of volume. You do this with a pencil, either its point or side, pressing lightly or harder. Basically, volume is created by the manipulation of light and dark, called "value" in drawing.

Photographs as subject

Black-and-white photographs are good subjects to draw when exploring volume because they break down the three-dimensional color world into two-dimensional lights and darks. Begin by identifying the light and dark variations in a black and white photo of a person or object. Also, try to identify the light source and direction. For example, is the light coming from the left side, causing the right side to be more in shadow? Is it shining straight at the subject, washing light evenly over all the parts of the image? Draw the outline of the object and then fill in the range of light and dark values that you see. I suggest using hard and soft pencils and drawing erasers.

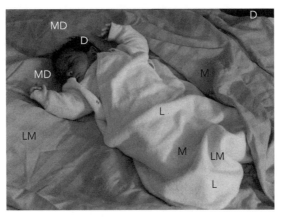

Values: L=light LM=light-medium M=medium MD=medium-dark D=dark

Three-dimensional subject

Select a simple, even, light-toned subject such as an egg, natural wood block, or ball. To exaggerate the values so you can see them better, place a strong light on the subject. Draw a faint outline of the shape. Then fill in the outline using the side of your pencil, showing the darker and lighter areas you observe. Create the lightest value first, then darkest values, then middle tones.

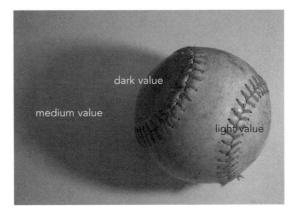

Scribble variation

Looking at either a photo or a real object, draw an outline of the object. Then create a range of dark to light values by building up loose scribbles. As you move your hand freely, thick, dense lines will create darker areas and thin, spare lines, lighter areas.

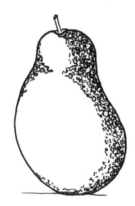

Adding energy

Quick sketches

Working fast, preferably with a soft pencil (or charcoal pencil), try to follow the lines of whatever you are observing to capture its overall shape in just a few lines. When learning to draw, we can become too tight with our lines. Drawing quickly and loosely is important as a warm-up for gesture drawing or to simply get familiar with a subject before launching into a longer drawing. Try to capture the sense of the shape in less than a minute. You are not looking for detail; rather, focus on just capturing the lines. Work on large newsprint if you can, so that your whole arm can make loose, large strokes. You can also add challenge by limiting the number of lines used: *Let's see if we can draw this vase in four strokes.*

Blind contour drawing

Choose a three-dimensional subject to draw (your other hand is a good subject). Draw the outside and inside edges or contours without looking at your drawing as you work and without lifting your pencil from the paper. With the subject of a hand, for example, you are studying both its outline and the inner wrinkles and folds of the fingers and skin.

As you and the students get used to looking really carefully, you can try doing "peek" versions, glancing once or twice at your paper during the drawing. Although contour drawing does not produce the accurate, detailed realism of general observational drawing, it gives excellent practice in looking hard at something and getting your hand to reproduce what your eyes see. Often, the naturalism and energy that this process generates spills over into your observational drawings.

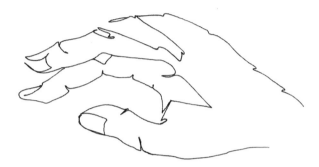

Drawing people

Many times the subject you wish to represent includes the human form, which, like any other subject, can be broken down into its parts. A few tried-and-true methods for representing both the gesture and form of the figure are listed below, for use alone or in combination.

The gesture: capturing the figure in movement

Action stick figures

While looking at a model or a drawing of a person, draw the figure as accurately as you can using only lines to follow the position of the subject. Look for joints or areas where the body bends for clues to capturing the pose.

Gesture drawing

This is a less analytical, more expressive version of figure drawing, using quick, flowing curved lines. Working fast, preferably with charcoal or a soft pencil, try to capture the overall pose with loose, quick hand movements, doing a drawing from start to finish in thirty seconds to one minute. Large paper is preferred as it allows for looser movement. A variation on this method is to try to capture the entire figure using just five lines.

Reflecting on your drawings

Spread out a few gesture drawings you have done and look at them, or gather students into a circle and put a bunch of gesture drawings in the middle (no names). Get a discussion going: *What do you notice about the lines in these drawings? What do they express about the subject?* Compare a gesture drawing of a person with a studied observational drawing: *What differences and similarities do you see between them?*

The form: capturing the proportions of the figure

Building up with shapes

Identify the basic parts of the body as simple shapes (circles, ovals, triangles, etc). Draw the different shapes, working down from the head—roughly an oval for the head, then a square or rectangle for the neck, etc. This method works well laid over an action stick figure drawing. You are aiming at correct proportions (for example, arms that hang down past the thigh, legs that are a little less than half the length of the whole body).

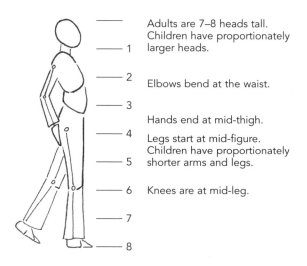

Adults are 7–8 heads tall. Children have proportionately larger heads.

Elbows bend at the waist.

Hands end at mid-thigh.

Legs start at mid-figure. Children have proportionately shorter arms and legs.

Knees are at mid-leg.

Drawing the human head

You can make a simple, accurate drawing of the human head when you break the process down into several steps. Once you understand these first steps, you can begin to make specific adjustments to capture the subtle differences among real faces. Artist Usry Alleyne wrote and illustrated the following step-by-step guide to drawing a realistic human head.

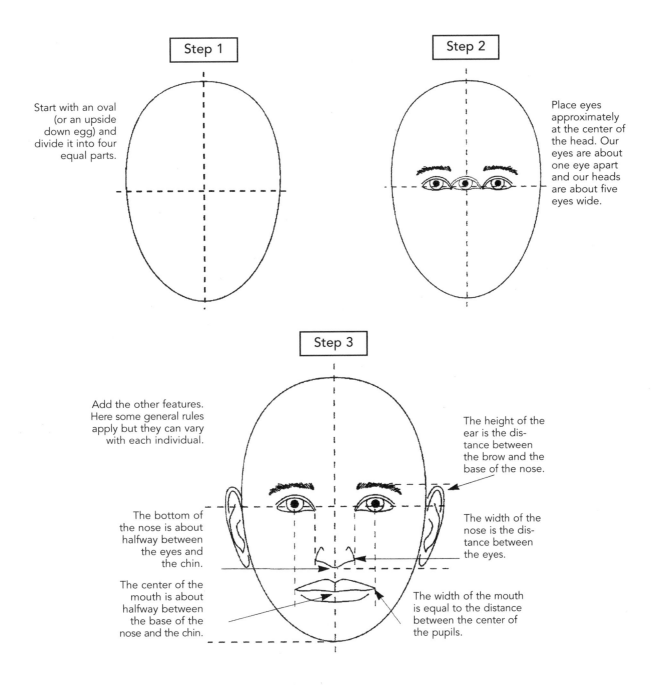

Step 1

Start with an oval (or an upside down egg) and divide it into four equal parts.

Step 2

Place eyes approximately at the center of the head. Our eyes are about one eye apart and our heads are about five eyes wide.

Step 3

Add the other features. Here some general rules apply but they can vary with each individual.

The height of the ear is the distance between the brow and the base of the nose.

The bottom of the nose is about halfway between the eyes and the chin.

The width of the nose is the distance between the eyes.

The center of the mouth is about halfway between the base of the nose and the chin.

The width of the mouth is equal to the distance between the center of the pupils.

Step 4

Once all of the details are in place, definition can be given to the face. Cheek bones, a chin, and hair can be added.

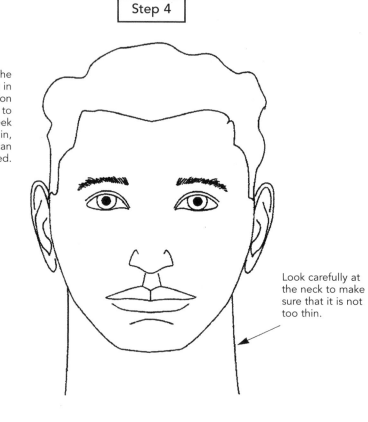

Look carefully at the neck to make sure that it is not too thin.

Step 5

Variations in age can be achieved by simply changing the proportions of the facial features.

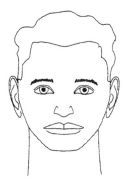
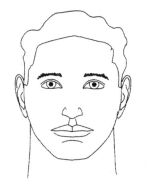
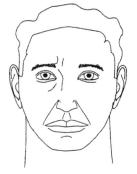

Here the face appears to be younger because the eyes are below the center of the head.

Here the face appears to be older because of a slightly wider neck, longer nose, and bigger chin.

Here the face appears to be older because some folds were added to the skin and the hair line was moved up.

Draw While You Teach

The fact that many children, even those who have good language skills, do not absorb information through verbal lectures and discussions alone is strong reason for all of us to teach with a marker or chalk in our hands. We wouldn't think of teaching how to solve an arithmetic problem merely by talking about it. We write the numbers as we say them, so that everyone can see how we set and solve the problem.

The use of exclusively, or even primarily, verbal or numerical language limits many students' capacity to form mental images. And without mental images, learners fail to internalize the information and ideas they are hearing. For some of our students, seeing is understanding. When they are doing their homework or taking a test, they need to form a mental image of the givens for a problem so they can manipulate those images and find their way to a solution. I use that method myself when I have no algorithm to solve a math problem.

Teachers who use images in addition to verbal or numerical language are much more likely to reach everyone in the class. It doesn't matter if your quick sketch of the protagonist of the story is simply a stick figure or a simplified icon. It provides the children an anchor while they try to answer your question about the hero: *Why do you think John ran away from home?* Maybe you can manage to show feet running. Maybe all that you add will be thought bubbles around a quickly drawn face to represent the children's ideas about the character's motivation. In either case, their eyes will be riveted to the drawing as they focus on the more abstract question and its possible answers.

So, draw while you teach. Keep the board or chart paper handy to make it as easy as possible to create some kind of visual to help focus attention, and students will soon take for granted that you will give them something to look at while you speak to them. Perhaps they will draw when *they* speak to the group or a partner, or draw while solving a problem on a test or planning a project. This will help them think, keep them grounded. Give your drawings to your students like a present—from one hard-working learner to another.

WORK CITED

Edwards, Betty. 1989. *Drawing on the Right Side of the Brain: A Course in Enhancing Creativity and Artistic Confidence*. Los Angeles: J. P. Tarcher.

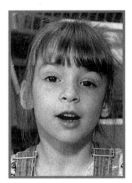

Getting Comfortable with Music

We've got the whole globe in our hands.
We've got the whole globe in our hands.
We've got the whole globe in our hands.
We've got the whole globe in our hands.
We've got North and South America in our hands.
We've got Europe, Asia, Africa in our hands.
We've got Australia and Antarctica in our hands.
We've got the whole globe in our hands.

Music can inspire and enliven any curriculum area. A recording of instrumental music can provide a spark for a writing project or background to quiet reading. Songs—either recorded or sung by the children—can bring a culture or period of history to life. Rhythmic counting-songs or chants can help children learn math skills and concepts. In Chapters 9 through 12 you'll find many examples of music used in various ways to teach the curriculum. In this chapter, I'll focus on group music making, particularly singing and making rhythms. As with all of the arts media discussed in this book, children and teachers will find it helpful to practice making music together before they use music for learning in curriculum areas. The suggestions offered below will help you bring music into the classroom in a way that feels safe and happy.

Singing

For as long as anyone can remember, children have sung songs and chants that they inherited from the children before them. In many cases nobody knows what the words mean anymore—or even if they were designed to make sense. Non-sense has always had a safe place in the hearts of children. Why do we sing? Singing lifts spirits, builds community, helps memory, enriches understanding, and oxygenates the brain! Why not sing?

Nevertheless, when I go from room to room or down the halls of elementary schools, except in the kindergartens, I don't hear children singing very often. Maybe teachers think there's not enough time to sing. But it only takes a couple of minutes to sing a song, so I wonder if for a lot of teachers the real reason is nervousness about singing with their students. Jo Devlin, our song leader at Origins summer workshops, says to teacher-participants, "Probably 75% of you are sitting there believing that you can't sing. Somebody told you that when you were in second grade or in the church choir, and it's not true! It's not best if you 'just move your lips, dear!'"

What teaches people to sing is singing. In many cultures where singing is a way of life, everyone sings because that is what you do—from early childhood throughout your life, every day, many times in the day. What we're talking about here is what Jo calls "casual" singing—the kind you just open your mouth and do—in the shower, in the car, with friends and family. You do it because it's a natural expression of your human capacity for song. So begin now by singing with your students.

The following are questions that are frequently asked by teachers who attend our Origins workshops. I hope the answers will help you get started.

What steps do I take to introduce a song?

If it's an old favorite like *Row, Row, Row Your Boat,* all who know it might sing it together right from the beginning. If not:

1. You sing the song first.

2. You sing a line and the children echo the line.

3. Everyone sings the song together all the way through a couple of times.

Repeat each step as many times as necessary until everyone sings it pretty well.

Can I use a recording of the song instead of singing it solo?

Yes, as a first step, play the recording (singing along with it to build your own confidence). Then have everyone sing along the second and third times. You can keep using the recording for a while. Then try it on your own—the children and you will hear yourselves much more clearly and will build confidence in unaccompanied singing. After a few repetitions, the strongest singers in the group will begin to carry the song.

How can I remember the tune?

If you don't remember the tune, listen to the recording again or ask the person from whom you learned the song to sing it for you. I usually record a friend singing a song, so that I can listen to it repeatedly. It takes me anywhere from five to fifteen times hearing and singing a song to be able to remember it days later. At this point (after fifty years) I have probably a couple of hundred songs that I've learned and memorized. Some I can sing without hesitation; others I need a quick reminder, and then I've got it again.

How do I know what note to start on?

When I'm singing with five- to eight- or nine-year-olds, I think of the note I would normally start on, given my adult voice, and then pitch it up to a point that is a little high for me, which should be just about right for young vocal cords. Older students might be able to sing in a range that's closer to the adult range. In either case you might need to try out different starting notes until you see where most in the group are comfortable.

Identify the first note of the song, either by singing the first word or by singing the first note with an "oo" (as in "moo") sound and having the class repeat it until everyone is singing the same note. When Jo Devlin begins a song, she often gives a direction to the group in a one-note monotone—the very same note that begins the song and that everyone has just been practicing: *Starting on this nohhhte—readyyy?* The practice on the first note together, along with this cuing, really helps the song go well.

How fast should we sing?

This is a choice that you and the children make. When you are first learning the song, go more slowly, and then pick up the tempo as you become familiar with it. Kindergartners and first graders, in general, sing more comfortably at a slower pace, while fifth graders may feel that a song isn't fun unless you sing it at a fast clip. Certainly some songs are at their best when you whirl through them.

How do we all stay together?

Somebody must keep the tempo for the group. At first, you indicate the pace by making a large, simple gesture with your hand (for example a closed or flat hand moving up and down in front of your body) so the children can easily watch you. You are the metronome, keeping the time for everyone.

Children can practice leading in their seats by making the hand motions along with you, but you remain the leader, no matter what their hands are saying. Eventually, children can take turns being the leader and keeping the tempo with these large, simple gestures, but they should do this one at a time. Two or more leaders will create confusion, even in rounds, because it is so hard to stay together. In the confusion, people will end up singing at different tempos and you'll have a muddled sound.

What if it sounds like a big mess?

It might be that the group is not together on the beat in the song. If so, start again by setting the tempo and keeping that same tempo clear with hand motions. It might be that the song is too complex for the group to handle at that time. Keep it simple—stick to songs with simple melodies and lots of repetition at first. Then try the trickier ones later.

But probably the most important thing to do is laugh. Then you can try again, perhaps get your music teacher in to help, go back to it another time on your own, or just ditch it! Don't let *it ditch you* and your determination to make music a part of your learning community.

Fitting Music into Your Day

The goal is to get comfortable enough with music that it can become one of the ways students learn and share curriculum content. But to get to that point, everyone will need some practice, which means finding moments during the day when you can make a little music.

Transition times

Transition times are the perfect opportunity for songs and rhythmic cheers and chants, many of which come with hand or whole body movements that can smooth out difficult moments.

Dum Dum Da Da, for example, is a rhythmic chanting, patting song that can be done with children standing in a circle or in line. The teacher begins by chanting *Dum, dum, da da, da da,* making movements in an AA BB pattern—for example:

> *Dum* [clap hands once], *dum* [clap hands once]

> *da da* [said in double time while you pat knees once] *da da* [double time and pat knees once]

The students then repeat the chant with the accompanying movements. You can vary the speed as well as the movements and volume. Try going from small motor movements such as snapping fingers to whole body movements such as touching toes and jumping high in the sky. Or perhaps from silent to loud and back to silent again. You can end this game with gentle, silent motions (such as tapping your shoulders or nodding your head) as a way of signaling that the game is over and it's time to move on to the next activity.

There are hundreds of songs and activities like this. And there are many resources to help you develop a repertoire, such as Jean Feldman's *Transition Time* (for primary grades, but many can be adapted for intermediate use as well) and Sara Bernstein's *Hand Clap!: "Miss Mary Mack" and 42 Other Hand-Clapping Games for Kids* (for upper elementary students). For more information about these and other music resources, please see the Resources section at the end of the book.

Greetings

To start off a day with music, greet each other with a song or rhythmic chant, such as one of these below.

Jump Shamador

Jump Shamador, a call-and-response song that can either be sung or rhythmically chanted, is a lively way to begin a day:

Children stand in a circle, with one child in the middle. The group begins the greeting, filling in the name of the child who is standing in the middle:

> [G]roup: Good morning to you, _____.

> [C]hild: Good morning to you, too.

G: What is your intention?

C: I want to be a _____ [dancer, pilot, basketball player, etc.]

G: You *can't* be a _____!

C: I *will* be a _____!

G: Well jump Shamador my darling, jump Shamador my dear!

As the group sings or chants the preceding line, the child in the center begins to skip or hop or run around the inside of the circle, usually making a motion related to the intended occupation, while the other children clap and continue to sing or chant the line in a rhythmic, quick beat.

After a few repetitions, the child exchanges places with someone in the circle while the group whispers:

Jump Shamador!

Jump Shamador!

Jump Shamador!

The group then sings the song again and so on around the circle.

Jeremy Nellis and his K–1 students at New City School
in Minneapolis greet each other with song and movement.

Rhythm Greeting

Older children might enjoy this greeting:

With the students seated in a circle, establish a four-beat rhythm by snapping fingers, clapping, or slapping hands on knees. When everyone is comfortably and easily keeping the beat, the whole group says the following, in time with the rhythm:

Say your first name,

And when you do,

We'll say your first name back to you.

The student who begins the greeting then says his/her first name on the first beat. The group snaps or claps beats two, three, and four, and says the student's first name on the next beat (beat one again):

Student: Johnny [2 - 3 - 4]

Group: Johnny [2 - 3 - 4]

Now the group repeats the opening chant, "Say your first name…" Johnny's neighbor then says her/his first name, and the group repeats it, and so on around the circle.

Activity break

Music is also great for a quick activity break. Start with a simple song that you already know and the children can learn and enjoy quickly, such as *Row, Row, Row Your Boat* or *My Bonny Lies Over the Ocean.*

For children in grades K–3, have everyone sing *My Bonny Lies Over the Ocean.* Whenever words beginning with a "b" are sung, children alternate between sitting and standing. For example: "My Bonny [stand] lies over the ocean. My Bonny [sit] lies over the sea…"

The words to the song are:

My Bonny lies over the ocean.

My Bonny lies over the sea.

My Bonny lies over the ocean.

Oh bring back my Bonny to me.

Bring back,

Bring back,

Bring back my Bonny to me, to me.

Bring back,

Bring back,

Bring back my Bonny to me.

My Bonny Lies Over the Ocean can also be adapted for use with older students. For example, ask children born in certain months (or with more than four letters in their first name or who like vanilla/chocolate) to stand or lift their arms or do some other gesture with the first "b" and those in other months (or other category) make their gesture beginning on the second "b". The children can make up endless variations, play with categories, and get some exercise, all at the same time!

You can build in some extra fun in other songs by adding little games to them. For example, sing *Row, Row, Row Your Boat* as a "diminishing" song. First sing the song in its entirety; then sing it seventeen more times (that takes only a minute or two), and lop off one word from the end of the song each time you sing it, so that at the end, the group sings a one-word verse, "Row!" and laughs.

There are many more such simple, playful songs and versions of songs. For example, in *A Sailor Went to Sea* (K–3), you salute on "sea" and "see":

A Sailor went to sea, you see

To see what he could see, you see

But all that he could see, you see

Was the bottom of the deep blue sea, sea, sea!

Sing if you know the tune, make a tune up if you don't know it, or chant. Start slowly and repeat until everyone gets the idea. Then speed it up, faster and faster, until you end with most people making a mess of it again!

With older children, who might be wary of singing, particularly early in the year when they're still getting to know each other, you can loosen things up and get them used to making sounds together and using their voices flexibly by doing an activity called *Pass the Sound.* Children sit in a circle. The person who begins the activity makes a sound and passes it to the next person in the circle, who first imitates and then gradually changes the sound. The second person then passes the new sound to the third person, and so on around the circle.

Building Your Repertoire

To build your repertoire, think of songs you learned in childhood, silly songs you sang with friends or family. Look for ones with gestures and body movements or joke songs like *Keep on the Sunny Side,* where the little ditty is interspersed with riddles and knock-knock jokes volunteered by the children. In the Resources section you'll find a list of songbooks, most of which have an accompanying tape or CD to help you learn the songs.

Rounds and call-and-response songs are two kinds of songs that are fun to include in your repertoire.

Rounds

Rounds are a great way to introduce singing in parts. In a round, everyone sings the same melody, but they sing it in a "staggered" way, thus creating harmony. Some of the simple songs already in your repertoire can be sung as rounds. For example, *Little Tommy Tinker* and *London's Burning* are lots of fun because in addition to singing round-style, the singers make the gestures in something like a musical version of a "wave."

If you haven't led your class in singing rounds before, *Row, Row, Row Your Boat* is a good place to start. First you need to divide the group into sections. Use two at first, three after you are comfortable with two parts. Tell each section to come in after the preceding section sings "boat." Start the first group: "Row, row, row your boat …." Point to the second group at their moment of entry, and start singing with them: "Row, row, row your boat…." Once the two groups are going, concentrate on keeping everyone singing at the same tempo with your large, simple hand motions.

Tradition says that you sing the song as many times as there are groups, so if it's a two-group round, sing the song through twice; if three groups, sing the song three times. If you are running out of time, just sing it through twice anyway. You'll still have fun, and you'll get to lunch on time!

Sing a simple round again and again, as long as it's still fun. If you want to try another round, practice singing the song in unison before you break it into parts. The books in the Resources section will give you lots of other ideas for rounds.

Call-and-response

Call-and-response songs are fun and lively. One of the world's oldest and most familiar variations is the one we use to call to one another at some distance: "Ma—ry!" "Wha—at?" "Dinner's ready!" "O—kay!" The structure simply requires one voice to sing or say a phrase, the "call," and then another voice "responds" or "answers." The two voices can keep going back and forth, or the caller can address the call to another person, who can respond with a musical phrase the same as or different from the first.

For example, in the following greeting song for grades K–2, the whole class sings the "call" and each individual responds in turn:

Where is _____?

(sung to the tune of *Frere Jacques*)

[G]roup: Where is _____? Where is _____?

[S]tudent: Here I am. Here I am.

G: How are you today, sir/ma'am?

S: Very well, I thank you.

G: We're glad you're here. We're glad you're here.

Making Rhythms

You and the children can also make music together by focusing on rhythm, creating sound and rhythm compositions either vocally or with simple percussion instruments such as river stones.

The two call-and-response activities, *Juby's Hat* and *Joe, Joe from Kokomo,* written by Jo Devlin for grades 3–8, use body percussion to establish a four-beat rhythm.

Juby's Hat

This call-and-response includes body percussion and verbal improvisations. Participants sit in a circle and establish a steady four-beat rhythm, patting thighs. To be sure all players are clear about the rhythm, all count "1-2-3-4" aloud a few times and then start patting.

[G]roup: Juby this and Juby that,

Juby wears a stylin' hat!

[S]tudent: Juby's hat has [asparagus]!

[You can maintain the rhythm when the players speak, or stop and pick it up again when all speak.]

G: Juby this and Juby that,

Juby wears a stylin' hat!

S: Juby's hat has asparagus and [bananas]!

G: Juby this and Juby that,

Juby wears a stylin' hat!

S: Juby's hat has asparagus, bananas, and [carrots]!

G: Juby this and Juby that,

Juby wears a stylin hat!

And so on down through the alphabet, with each player repeating all of the things already on Juby's hat before adding to the list. The game can be made simpler by omitting the alphabetical order, the category of things to add, or the cumulative aspect. Then it is a simple rhythmic call-and-response. Either way, it's fun.

Joe, Joe from Kokomo

In this activity, the whole group chants the call, asking individual students to improvise a rhythm response that the whole group then echoes. Establish a steady four-beat rhythm, patting thighs. To be sure all players are clear about the rhythm, all count "1-2-3-4" aloud a few times while patting thighs. Don't speed up and go too fast!

Group: DeShon DeShon from Kokomo

Stole the show—now what do you know?!

DeShon: I know this and I know that,

I know where the rhythm's at:

/ / / /   / / / / [He improvises an 8-beat rhythm.]

Group: / / / /   / / / / [Everyone echoes DeShon's rhythm.]

The game continues around the circle, with the group repeating the chant and putting in a different person's name each time.

Stone rhythms

If you invest about ten dollars in a box of polished river stones, usually sold at craft stores, you will have a musical instrument that enables you and the children to do call-and-response and other rhythms with innovation and spontaneity.

Everyone in the circle gets two stones. First, with the children, explore the stones and what they can do. I usually begin by asking students, "What do you notice about these stones?" After a few students have shared their observations, I'll ask for a volunteer to demonstrate using the stones to make a sound. For example, Neil might demonstrate tapping the stones together. Then we all tap the stones together. A second volunteer, Carlotta, might demonstrate tapping the stones on the carpet and we all try this. I'll then ask the students, "What did you notice about Neil's sound? About Carlotta's? How do the two sounds compare?" During this initial exploration we'll also talk about how to take care of the stones so they stay in good shape. Once the children understand how to use the stones carefully and effectively, the class can improvise rhythms together in a number of ways:

- **You can make a variety of rhythms with your stones and the children can echo you each time.**

  You can make the exercise more challenging by giving the children longer sequences and by giving them one rhythm, pausing, then a second rhythm to see if they can listen hard and remember the two rhythms accurately.

- **You can go around the circle, with each child making a rhythm that the class as a whole echoes.**

- **You can give a "call" rhythm to a student who can answer with a rhythm of her/his own.**

  Then you give your original call again and the whole class answers with the student's rhythm. You go around the circle giving the same call to each child, but receiving a different answer each time. Later, after practice, you might ask a student to be the caller.

- **Students can combine a group rhythm with passing stones around the circle.**

  For example, you and the students each hold two stones, one in each hand. Everyone clicks the two stones together four times, taps the two stones on the floor four times, clicks the two stones together again four times, and then taps once on the floor in front of the person to the right. In this last movement, everyone leaves their stones in front of the person on the right and receives new stones from the person on the left.

  Variation: Pass one stone and keep one stone.

The possible patterns of calling, echoing, and passing are limitless. You and the students can challenge each other to listen well, count beats as you listen, describe the pattern sequences as they are created, develop the memory capacity to repeat longer sequences, and increase hand-eye coordination with tricky passing arrangements. The benefits to skill development are many.

Small group rhythm ensembles

The idea in rhythm ensembles is for different voices in a small group to make different sounds, but all the sounds come together in a coordinated whole. Everyone has the chance to be creative, but the group sound is the final goal.

Name ensembles are a good place to begin. In small groups of three to five, each person says his/her name using whatever rhythm s/he wishes within four beats. I, for example, might say "Linnnnnnnnda," and stretch out my name for four beats. Robert may use a sharp, short, repeating version of his name: "Bob Bob Bob Bob." Demetrius may say his name stressing the last syllable: "De me tri us." Honore may stress the first syllable of her name and then rest for a beat: "Hon [rest] or re." When everyone in the ensemble chants their names at the same time, four or five times, we'll get an interesting, perhaps beautiful, medley of names that we can perform for the rest of the class.

You could also use sounds instead of actual words. The sounds can be vocalized sounds, body percussion snaps and claps, or percussion instruments such as rhythm sticks, jingle bells, triangles, castanets, drums, maracas—or any of the dozens of inexpensive rhythm-making devices you can buy or make. For example, empty film canisters with a little rice or some beans in them make gentle rattles. The small groups can also use the simple polished stones described above, for quiet click and tap sounds.

In this call-and-response rhythm activity, five- and six-year-olds
focus hard so they can repeat each other's improvised rhythms.

The small groups can use a combination of vocalizations and rhythm-makers or choose the same sort of sound with variations. The groups get a few minutes to create and practice their short (about thirty-second) arrangements, and then they perform for one another. Such group work requires the same qualities needed in any successful collaboration—good listening, sensitivity to the group, and creativity balanced by teamwork.

Banding Together

Where does all this rhythm-making and singing together get us? Here's what happened when one fifth/sixth grade teacher, Karen Randall, turned to music to help a particularly challenging class. Karen came to my house for dinner one fall evening, along with several other teacher friends. "My class this year doesn't seem interested in school at all," she said. "They grump a lot, don't get along, and don't want to work."

The dinner group sympathized. "Do they show interest in anything?" one teacher asked.

"They love singing together," Karen replied.

A couple of months later I called Karen, and she reported that singing together had really made a difference in the group. It was as if the cooperation necessary to sing together had extended into the rest of the day. There was more interest in work and fewer quarrels and behavior issues.

One day after singing at morning meeting a student said, "We sound so good—too bad we can't make a recording!" For years, Karen has organized thematic units around areas of student interest, and for her this was like a door opening. She and the children began to think about what might be necessary to produce a CD of their repertoire of songs. They brainstormed songs they would sing,

Some of the original CD covers (left) made by students in Karen Randall's fifth/sixth grade class, and a draft of the CD liner notes (right).

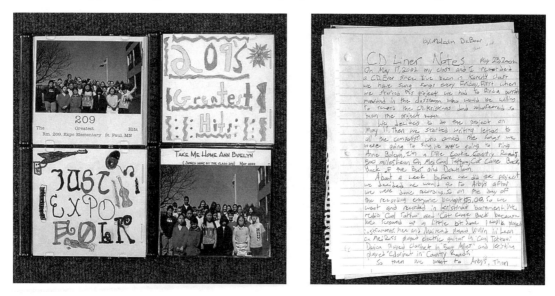

discussing the meanings of the lyrics. Many were folk songs that illuminated various periods of American history. They discussed the role that music plays in people's lives. They visited an exhibit on *Music in Minnesota,* took notes, interviewed the curator, and gave short reports to each other on ways that music is part of people's lives. They pared down the list of songs.

They discussed copyright law and researched the companies who owned the rights to the songs they wanted to sing. They used the Internet to search for addresses and phone numbers. They wrote persuasive business letters requesting information about permissions and requesting donations. They interviewed a local record producer about the steps artists must go through to make CDs and how they are marketed. They practiced on their own and with musicians who had volunteered to accompany them. Finally there was the recording session with a student's father in the family basement, the brainstorming of titles, the making of individual CD covers using digital photos and drawings, the writing of liner notes, the list of songs and credits, and the CD release party!

This music-centered project helped a cranky class, at odds with itself and the world, to get interested in school and enjoy one another. It also motivated the students to develop a variety of skills: using computers, researching, comprehending text, note-taking, interviewing, making oral reports, writing business letters, and cataloging.

This was an unusual circumstance and an elaborate project, but it illustrates not only the many links between music and curriculum content but also how making music can help students become a productive community.

CHAPTER 5

Getting Comfortable with Movement

If you're happy and you know it clap your hands!
If you're happy and you know it clap your hands!
If you're happy and you know it then your face
    will really show it.
If you're happy and you know it clap your hands!

The brain is a "system of systems," and most of it is activated during physical activity, says Eric Jensen in *Arts with the Brain in Mind.* (Jensen 2001, 72 & 95) Movement is essential to learning. It awakens, activates, integrates, and anchors new information and experience into our neural networks. It is movement, not sitting still in chairs, that maximizes our students' abilities to think and remember.

Movement is natural to children—we don't have to coax them to do it. In fact, a great deal of teacher energy is spent trying to get them to *stop* doing movement when it's the wrong kind at the wrong time in the wrong place. Children need our help in knowing when and how to move in school. Using your body skillfully takes guided opportunities and practice, and like the other art forms, has a big payoff in confidence, attention, self-expression, and understanding.

There are many ways and times to use movement in the classroom: to teach content, to practice social skills, to stimulate energy, and to build community. Movement can help your students internalize what they are learning, imprinting upon their bodies the social and academic lessons of the day. But before movement can become a constructive part of the classroom routine, you'll need to spend some time teaching and practicing how to move with self-control.

Guidelines for Moving in the Classroom

Ironically, it is just when students are acting goofy and need redirection every few minutes—in short, when you are having a "bad" day or lesson—that they need movement the most. If you could give them an opportunity to move, to get their wiggles and nervousness out, you might be able to save the day. But many teachers avoid movement for fear that the class will get out of hand, especially if the children seem restless already.

The best way I know to prepare children for any movement activity in the classroom is to proactively model and practice how to move responsibly and with self-control (see Chapter 2 for information about modeling).

Teach, model, and practice how to maintain personal space

When you begin movement activities, especially with young children, you'll notice that the spaces between people have a way of disappearing because the children tend to clump together as they move. So the crucial thing is for them to learn to maintain their personal space while moving and not intrude upon anyone else's space. To work on this:

- Clear a space in the classroom.

  Better yet, use an all-purpose room or gym. Have the children spread out in the space.

- Ask the children to stand so they have plenty of room between each other.

  They should be able to extend their arms out from their sides and move their arms without banging into anyone or anything. If you are doing this in the limited space of a classroom, you will probably need to have students keep their arms fairly close to their sides rather than fully extended.

- Invite them to look around the space and make sure they have as much room as they can within their boundaries.

- Ask for a volunteer to demonstrate a small movement while staying within his personal boundaries.

  For example:

  Leonard, will you reach up as high as you can? Now reach towards the floor. Now lie down on the floor. Can you try swinging your arms a little, taking care that you do not touch anyone else? I see that you had enough room to make gentle swings without bumping into anyone.

  You may choose to have two or more children do such demonstrations with your prompting and then ask the entire group to do these movements.

- Now, ask one child to demonstrate how to walk around slowly, with hands by his sides, not bumping into anyone.

  As the child demonstrates, change the directions slightly, asking the child to stretch his arms out and still not bump into anyone. After the child finishes modeling, talk with the children about what they noticed. Here's a sample of a conversation after Anthony modeled moving from one place to another:

  "He didn't bump into anyone," a child says.

  "Anthony, what did you do to make sure that you wouldn't bump into anyone?" the teacher asks.

  "I looked where I was going and I moved a different way if I was headed for someone."

  "Will you show us how you can safely change direction when you need to?"

- Next, ask two people to move at the same time.

  If Rochelle and Jessica are doing the moving, the rest of the class should watch Rochelle and Jessica carefully and be ready to describe how they keep space around themselves so they won't bump into each other or anyone else.

- Finally, ask everyone to practice.

  Tell them to be sure to move as carefully as Leonard, Anthony, Rochelle, and Jessica. You can establish a rhythm with slow beats on a drum or other percussion instrument or by clapping. Ask the children to move to the beat—slowly—and to watch out of the corners of their eyes so they don't bump into each other.

Tell the children that they have been exploring their "personal space," a little bubble of safety that protects them and everyone else during movement activities, and that soon they are going to have a chance to try moving around to different tempos. But before you have the children do this, ask them to say what they need to pay attention to in order for the activity to be safe and fun for everyone. Establish what will happen if someone forgets to move safely: *If anyone forgets and bumps into anyone else, that person will stand or sit by me for a couple of minutes and watch the group move, so that he or she learns how to move more safely.*

After you've established a clear standard for paying attention, watching carefully, and moving in a controlled manner, give the children a chance to show that they can do this well. Give them a variety of tempos, slower ones first, then picking up speed when they demonstrate their ability to maintain self-control. If the movers are doing well, give them a really rapid tempo to follow, then bring the beat down gradually to a very slow tempo, and then finally stop. You might use the signal, "Freeze!" so that the children can enjoy the pleasure of catching themselves in an active position and holding it.

At every point in this or any other group movement exercise, you are watching to make sure that everyone is following directions and moving appropriately. A student who speaks when you've asked for silence or goes too fast or does his own thing, might be losing self-control.

The moment you see a child losing self-control, give the child a reminder. If she continues the behavior, direct her to leave the group and sit in a quiet place to watch. (This is a process that needs to be modeled and practiced ahead of time.) To be sure that this redirection doesn't come across as punitive or shaming, use a matter-of-fact voice, without an edge of anger or sarcasm. The point of leaving the group is not for the child to feel bad about what she's done wrong; rather, it gives her an opportunity to calm down and regain self-control.

If a number of students are showing they cannot control themselves, ask yourself if the children need more ground work, either in practicing the movements, following instructions, or taking a break when they can't maintain self-control. If the answer is "yes," stop the movement exercise and practice the fundamentals with everyone again. Or you may decide that today is not the day: *I guess we weren't ready for moving together today. We'll practice a little tomorrow, and then see if we have the self-control we need to do more movement together.*

Three Basic Elements of Movement

In order to use movement to learn, students will need to become familiar with the three elements from which all movement is constructed: space, time, and energy. These are the building blocks—explore them with your students, and then you and they can use them to build skills and express and respond to concepts and facts in the curriculum.

In an open space have the children locate their own spaces. Then guide their exploration of space, time, and energy with movement directions. You can spread this exploration out over several sessions.

Space

Size of the space

Ask students to move around inside a tiny space, not much bigger than a circle around their feet. Now ask them to explore a slightly larger circle by walking around it. As they continue exploring a wider and wider area, they'll need to watch out for their neighbors and stay inside their own "bubble" of personal space. By the end of this part of the exploration, they can go anywhere in the room as long as they stay in their bubble of space and avoid bumping into other students' bubbles.

Levels of space

Say, "Freeze!" Tell students that when you say "melt," they're going to get a chance to explore the levels of the space in which they're standing. Say "melt" and then ask them to:

- Stretch upwards

- Bend their knees and find a middle level

- Get down as low as they can, close to the floor

Shapes of space

Ask students to stand tall and straight so that their bodies make a straight line. Now, ask a student to demonstrate making a curve with the body and then have everyone try making a curve. Ask students to try different shapes on their own. When all students have had a chance to try several shapes, say, "Freeze!" Then invite one half of the group at a time to look around and see all the shapes the other students have made.

Directions in space

Invite a student to demonstrate forward movement and then a careful backward movement. Ask the students who are watching to notice how the student makes sure he doesn't bump into anyone when he moves backwards. After a successful demonstration, everyone tries moving forward four steps, and then, looking over their shoulders first to make sure the path is clear, they try moving backwards four steps. They can also go sideways four steps, watching out for other people again. Finally, ask a student to demonstrate moving at a diagonal.

Pathways in space

To explore pathways in space, ask everyone to move in any direction in a straight line, then in a curved line, a circle, and finally a zigzag line. They can experiment with different combinations, perhaps moving to the beat of a drum. Ask them to notice how other people are moving and offer positive reinforcement for safe movement: *I see that people are remembering their bubbles and watching for others.*

Relationships to other people in space

Ask students to approach each other, being sure to maintain their own bubble of space. Now ask them to move apart from each other, then move around the room, sometimes close to others, sometimes apart. Ask them to notice when clumps of people gather and when they are more spread out. Finally, everyone finds a solitary space again and stands very, very still.

Time

You can explore time in relationship to movement by paying attention to varying speeds of travel around the room. Tell students that you'll establish a rhythmic beat (you can use a small drum, hand claps, a hand hitting a desk, etc.) and that they should follow the beat with their steps. Vary the beat so students can get used to a variety of speeds. Try a waltz rhythm (one, two, three) or marching (brisk, even tempo). Finally, ask students to walk around without a background rhythm, fast, medium, and slow.

Energy

To explore energy, you can ask students to use movement to express different qualities:

- **Strength**   *Walk around in a strong way.*

- **Weakness**   *Walk around showing how weak you feel.*

- **Heaviness**   *You weigh five hundred pounds—try to move your very heavy body.*

- **Lightness**   *Oh—all of a sudden you weigh almost nothing and can move like a feather in space!*

- **Smoothness**   *Pretend you are made of cream now and move smoothly as if you were being poured from a pitcher.*

- **Sharpness**   *Now you are made of sharp edges and you move like a knife in space.*

Then say, "Freeze!" Ask students to stay in one spot but move every part of their bodies. Then say "Freeze!" again. Next, ask children to move through space choosing some of these ways you have practiced. You can accompany them with a rhythmic beat. After they've had a couple of minutes to explore all these elements of movement, say "Freeze!" again. Briefly discuss what they've learned. For example, you might ask: *As you moved around the room, what kinds of movements did you notice other people doing?*

Or, instead of having a discussion you could end by taking a survey:

Raise your hand if you saw someone doing something, and then you began to do it.

Raise your hand if you did at least three different kinds of movements.

Now your students have the beginnings of a movement "vocabulary" which they can use to express any fact or idea. If students are retelling a story, they can use their movement vocabulary to represent the plot or show a character. If they are describing rivers or photosynthesis or plate tectonics, they can use their bodies more expressively and accurately to show the details. Your job is to provide some structure; theirs is to do the thing they love best—move—within that structure.

Daily Practice of Movement

There are many cultures in which formal education includes intervals of structured movement to stimulate the brain and address the need of young bodies to move. Eric Jensen suggests that if students are not in a good state to learn, teachers should consider using movement to reduce stress, regulate mood, and quicken mental reactions. (Jensen 2001, 100–101)

Following are two of my favorite movement disciplines for the classroom. The skilled practitioners who developed these two routines worked to design a daily practice that is quick (five minutes or less) and easy, and that releases tension and increases blood flow and body oxygen.

For both of these daily practices, you may decide to start with only a few movements, model and practice them, and then gradually build the sequence with the children. Another method would be to first demonstrate the entire sequence, with the students mirroring your movements as you go, and then practice as many of the individual pieces as you can in the time you have.

Loosen up

This is a practice from the traditions of Chinese medicine. It is based on the idea that gentle, circular movement through the body's range of motion stimulates blood flow and therefore energy. Jill Reshanov, a Shiatsu bodywork therapist, designed the following movement routine for teachers to use during brief classroom breaks.

Do these exercises, which are designed to move every joint in the body, in a slow, gentle, and relaxed manner. Do small rotations of the joints, gradually building in size over the course of weeks. Do the exercises daily and enjoy the energy they bring to you and the children. After you are familiar with the movements, the whole routine will take only three to five minutes.

(Photos by Usry Alleyne)

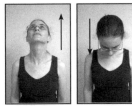 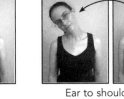 

Look up, look down (4x)   Look side to side (4x)   Ear to shoulder (4x)

 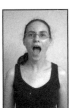  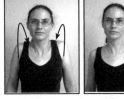

Half neck circles (4x)   Open and close mouth (4x)   Circle shoulders (4x) backwards and forward

  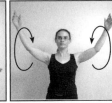 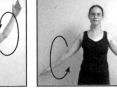 

Shrug (4x)   Small arm circles (4x) both directions   Big arm circles (4x) both directions

Circle elbows (4x) both directions

Circle wrists
(4x) both directions

Caterpillar fingers (4x)

Reach up
(1x) arms together

Alternate reaching (4x)

Reach forward (4x)
alternate arms

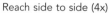

Reach side to side (4x)

Reach down (4x)
alternate arms

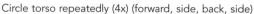

Circle torso repeatedly (4x) (forward, side, back, side)

Circle hips (4x)
(like a hulahoop)

 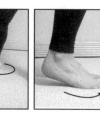   

Circle knees
(4x) both ways

Circle ankles
(4x) both ways

Rock and roll feet (4x)

Do the twist (4x)

   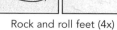 

Twist and flop arms
look behind (4x)

Hang from waist
dangle arms

Stand and roll up
supporting low back

Stand with
good posture

Yoga

The yoga tradition emphasizes control of breathing and slow stretching that increases body flexibility and awareness. Yoga has a calming effect that helps children center their energies and focus attention. My daughter Jessica Crawford teaches yoga classes for children and has introduced a series of exercises to teachers in our summer workshops. Like the *Loosen Up* series, yoga provides a quick interval of relaxation and refreshment that, by improving physical tone and breathing, will allow children to return to their studies with more focus and concentration. It also may offer your students an opportunity to begin a lifelong habit of daily movement practice to keep them healthier and happier as adults.

In order to do yoga effectively and safely, you'll need more instruction than I can offer here. For more information, please consult a book such as *Yoga for Children* (see Resources) or contact a local yoga teacher. The following photos show some common poses that are easy for children to do.

(Photos by Jo Devlin)

Hang

Rolling up

Mountain

Sun breath

Low "ha!"

Middle "ha!"

High "ha!"

Pause and receive

Windmill

Jiggle and shake

Half moon

Children moving well together is a beautiful sight. Once you see the spark that structured movement brings to the class and the boost to attentiveness, you will want to do more. Take it as slowly as you wish, but take it! Structured movement in the classroom directs the flow of children's enormous energy into channels for learning. Think of yourself as the gatekeeper and when the conditions are right and the need present, open the gates and move!

WORK CITED

Jensen, Eric. 2001. *Arts with the Brain in Mind.* Alexandria, VA: Association for Supervision and Curriculum Development (ASCD).

CHAPTER 6

Getting Comfortable with Theater

"You be the baby and I'll be the mom."

"Let's play store—I come in and you show me this doll and I buy it."

"The princess is locked in a dungeon, and her fairy godmother is looking for her. Who wants to be the fairy godmother?"

From early childhood on, much of children's play takes the form of pretending. We call this kind of play "make-believe," an interesting choice of words since it describes the effect on both audience and players. Everyone temporarily suspends disbelief, at least a little, and feels excitement about the new toy or pity for the lost princess.

Young children seem to be able to slide in and out of the willing suspension of disbelief necessary for absorption in a pretend life. But older ones need to storm the walls of self-consciousness. It's worth the climb because once on the other side, their eyes shine and their energy spikes. It is that shine and that energy we can co-opt for learning. But how do we help children—and ourselves—feel comfortable engaging in theater activities in the classroom, a possibly riskier setting than the living room or backyard? And how do we find the time to bring theater into an already crowded classroom life? In this chapter, we'll look at two ways to successfully introduce theater experiences into an ordinary busy day: theater games and storytelling.

Theater Games

The class stands in a circle. The teacher leans down and takes an invisible ball out of an invisible box. She places the imaginary ball very gently on the floor and closes the lid of the imaginary box. "I have a magic ball," she says, "and it can change its shape or size or anything about it. Watch."

She pretends to lift the ball and polish it, and then moves her arms apart as if it were growing larger and larger. Finally she offers to pass the ball to the person standing next to her. This person takes the ball, immediately bounces it in front of her a few times, and then passes it to the person next to her.

The ball travels around the circle. Sometimes it is a punching ball; sometimes it's twirled on a finger; one time it is popped in a mouth, chewed, and reappears as a bubble-gum bubble. Everyone watches each transformation. There are giggles, ooh's, oh no's!— the group is focused and enjoying itself. Each person participates, even the shy ones.

This is a theater game sometimes called *Energy Ball*. Done in a playful context, which minimizes fear, *Energy Ball* and other quick theater games can help students feel more comfortable performing in front of an audience—something they'll need to do throughout the year as they act out a role in a simulation, read aloud a poem they've written, or demonstrate their solution to a math problem.

Theater games are perfect as quick tension-breakers and community builders. They can fill an awkward few minutes in the schedule, offer closure to the day, or bring everyone together after a transition. Some theater games involve talking; others require silence. Some elicit individual performances; others call for group collaborations. Although you can adapt them to the front-of-the-room space, you'll want to play most of them in a circle, which becomes a theater-in-the-round. There are hundreds of games that involve some level of acting, probably the best known being *Charades*. In the Resources section, you'll find collections of theater games and activities.

How to introduce theater games

Before students engage in active theater games, they need to model and practice the procedures that are involved. They need to practice circling up in a careful, quick way. They need to practice taking turns, being an audience, and moving their bodies in space without bumping into others. They must work on stopping their activity at the signal for quiet and restraining their urge to blurt out and side-talk when others are talking.

They also need to understand the consequences of not following these rules, which might be leaving the activity for a few minutes to regain self-control or losing the privilege of doing that activity that day. But it's important to practice routines and discuss consequences for not following the rules before the activity begins, and to keep the tone of discussions non-punitive:

It is a hard thing to move around, talk, even laugh, and follow the rules at the same time, but you'll have opportunities to practice doing this so that you can act out stories and do fun theater games this year. If you have trouble with self-control, I'll stop the theater work and give you a chance to regain your self-control. I think you'll get very good at controlling yourselves even when you're excited.

When properly introduced, theater games offer students practice in self-control, which will be crucial to the success of more involved theater activities, to say nothing of life in general! Following are a few easy-to-learn, quick, adaptable theater games.

Pantomimes

Wink (Grades 2–8)

This simple pantomime is a good beginning for class theater games. All the students close their eyes while the teacher moves around the circle and taps one person to be the Winker. Students open their eyes and either sit quietly in their seats, or if they can handle it, begin to move around the room. The Winker can hypnotize people into sleep merely by winking at them, and tries to do so without being detected. When the Winker winks at someone, that child lies down and pantomimes sleep (sleepers can open their eyes to watch the action). Other children try to guess who the Winker is before she winks at them. If a child guesses wrong, he joins the sleepers. The game ends either when the Winker has put everyone to sleep or someone correctly guesses the identity of the Winker. The person who guesses correctly gets to pick the next Winker.

Transformation Walk (Grades K–8)

While music is playing, students walk freely around the circle (or around the room if there is space and they have good self-control). The teacher calls out a feeling, image, or idea for them to express as they walk—"light as a feather," "stones in your shoes," "itchy back," etc. When students have been walking for a few moments in a way that expresses that image, the teacher says, "Freeze!" They pause, holding that position. When the teacher tells them to melt, they begin walking normally again, and the teacher calls out another image, feeling, etc.

Variations: Set the pace with a drum or other percussion instrument, then vary the speed. You can do this activity in a large open space like a gym or outside, but be sure to mark the boundaries.

What Are You Doing? (Grades 2–8)

One person pantomimes an activity such as combing his hair. The person next to him asks, "What are you doing?" The person doing the activity answers by naming another activity, such as fishing. The person who asked then begins to pantomime fishing, and the next person in the circle asks, "What are you doing?" The game continues around the circle, with the answer to the question, "What are you doing?" always being different from the action being pantomimed. One caution is that the class needs to consider ahead of time what types of things are appropriate to pantomime in school.

Help! (Grades 2–8)

One person starts with a pantomime of making an effort at doing something. The second person asks, "Can I help you _____?" filling in what she thinks the first person is trying to do. The first person goes along with the stated task (even if it was not what he was doing), and the two complete the effort together. They end by the first person saying, "Thanks for your help!" and the activity moves to the next pair. Here's an example:

The first person pantomimes moving a heavy piece of furniture.

The second person asks, "Can I help you move that rock?" and they both pantomime trying to move a rock.

Machines (Grades 2–8)

This game requires team work so that each group can construct a collaborative pantomime. Groups of six or eight are assigned a machine, such as a washing machine, bus, or merry-go-round. The group's task is to become that machine. The groups are given two or three minutes to figure out how they will perform as their machine, and then each group demonstrates while the others watch and try to guess what machine is being pantomimed. You can also extend the group pantomimes to include natural phenomena such as mountains or waterfalls.

Improvisations

Name Game (Grades 1–8)

This exercise helps students take risks, so it's best to introduce it after a sense of community safety has developed and to ask that everyone participate. The first person says her name and then does an action that expresses who she is. A child who loves basketball, for example, might pantomime a hoop shot. This can be done either at her place in the circle or in the center of the circle, depending upon her choice or the teacher's assessment of what's best for the group. Then the rest of the students make the same gesture and repeat the student's name.

An extension of this game, which is appropriate for grades 3–8, is a version of *Concentration*. After everyone has introduced him or herself with an identifying gesture, one person does her gesture silently, and then does the gesture of someone else, and sits down. That second person, recognizing his own gesture, repeats it, does the gesture of someone else who is still standing, and then sits down. If, as the game goes on, students start forgetting the gestures, everyone still standing can repeat his or her gesture.

What Do I Do for a Living? (Grades 2–8)

One person leaves the room. The group decides what profession the person who is out of the room will have. When he returns, the group interacts with him, one by one, in ways that are appropriate for that profession. For example, if "It" is a gardener, people may interact by bringing him tools or seeds, by offering to help weed, or by buying produce from him. When "It" thinks he knows his job, he plays along to see if he's correct. If he is, that round comes to an end. If he's not, the group can continue interacting with him until he figures it out, or the teacher decides to move on.

Variation: You can adapt this activity for five- and six-year-olds by removing the guessing and selecting a child to be the worker:

Teacher: Daniel, what work will you do?

Daniel: Build a house.

Teacher: OK, Daniel is a house builder and we're going to bring him what he needs to build his house. Who has an idea about something you could give him that would help him? Megan?

Megan: A hammer.

Teacher: Yes—go give him his hammer, and we'll see what he does with it.

[Daniel pantomimes pounding with the hammer.]

Teacher: Diego?

Diego: Nails!

Teacher: Of course! He's got to have something to put things together with. Give him some nails and let's see what he does.

Storytelling

There are potentially many storytellers in the classroom: the children, visitors—and you, their teacher, who can use this form of theater as a powerful way to teach curriculum content. Storytelling captures students' attention and helps them increase their knowledge and develop their cognitive skills. When the facts are set in a narrative, students are more likely to remember them. When they try to figure out what's going to happen in the story, they are predicting. When they see that the houses made of straw and sticks get blown down by the wolf, they are using cause and effect. With pleasure, children are engaging in high-order thinking.

Many teachers bring stories about their own lives into the classroom—about children, pets, family experiences, etc. If a story has meaning for you, it will most likely have meaning for your students, so use these personal stories to help teach curriculum. As you plan lessons, look for the places where the topic in science or social studies or literature connects to your own life or the lives of people you know. Childhood memories, school memories, moments of strong emotion, moments of conflict, people you have loved, people who inspired you, trouble you've gotten into, animals you've known—these are some of the sources from your life that tie in with conflicts in history, for example, or with literature, or even with science. Connections that at first seem remote turn out to provide a memorable anecdote to which students can link their learning.

To teach principles of gravity, I could tell about a time when I lived on a hilly street with a trunk water runoff sewer at the bottom, and gravity was an annoying reality because we had to chase so many balls down the hill or retrieve them out of the runoff stream. To launch a study of plants, I've told the story of the "Victory Seeds" I enthusiastically planted under the drain spout in my back yard for three successive years during World War II, and my disappointment in their failure to sprout.

To ensure a successful performance, choose a story that you enjoy telling. Create a context for the story. How does it connect to what the students are studying or experiencing? What reminded you of it? Your audience will be more attentive when they have an idea of the point of the story.

Here are some other things to pay attention to as you get ready to tell stories:

Use your voice in a dynamic way

Use variations in timing, expression *("I do not un der stannnnd you sometimes, Charles"),* and volume. Don't be surprised if your voice changes from telling to telling, from story to story, from audience to audience. And don't forget to breathe and to speak clearly and precisely.

Add sounds

Expressive sounds in sentences can enhance the rhythm and create drama. *The forest was dark and the sounds scary—ooooh, ooooh, ooooh—what was that?!* Invite the audience to make sounds, speak words, gesture, or add clapping or snapping rhythms. Sing if the mood strikes you. Repeat key words and phrases for effect and have the audience echo them.

Keep eye contact with the audience

Don't look just at the people who seem to be listening to you. Establish rapport with the whole group by directing your story to everyone. But don't "scan" the room constantly—sometimes meet the eyes of individuals, linger for a moment, and then move on.

Let your body talk

All movement communicates. Move closer to your audience at times to establish intimacy and dramatize key moments. To make the story come alive, use facial expressions, hands, and various body postures when you are relaxed enough to do so. Not all stories need to be "acted out," however. Some stories are very effective when told simply and quietly as the teller sits in a chair. Even so, if you are usually a "sit and tell" storyteller, you could give movement a try now and then to see what energy it might bring to a story.

Involve the imagination

See your story as you tell it. Think about adding details that encourage your listeners to see, feel, hear, or taste what you are describing. Use exaggeration to add color. But stories don't need to be elaborate. Evocative stories can be told in just a few sentences, and your audience's imagination will fill them out.

Practice

Practice telling your story so you gain confidence. Practice with adults or children—you might get feedback about which part they liked best, and you can build on that.

Be yourself

Tell stories in a way that is natural for you. There are as many ways to tell stories as there are storytellers! Don't try to adopt a flamboyant style because you think that's what storytellers are supposed to do. Your comfort level will support the story and will provide a genuineness that your listeners will appreciate and relate to.

Student stories

The teacher is not the only storyteller in the room, of course. Each member of the class has stories that can contribute to everyone's learning. Children are very interested in each other, and from about age eight they begin to be more tuned in to what their peers think and say than to the words of the adults around them—the audience for children's stories in the classroom is a given.

There are many occasions for inviting stories during the school day, but one of the best times is during a daily morning gathering when students can sign up to share a story about an event in their lives. To keep the stories lively, encourage the storyteller to focus on a main idea, to elaborate with relevant and interesting details, and to keep the story short so there is time for questions and comments.

If children are guided to ask probing questions and give detail-rich answers, they can expect interesting narratives. This means you may wish to systematically discourage head-shaking, pointing, and mono-syllabic or one-word answers, and to model questions that bring out the details of the story. You can also specify the topic beforehand and have the group brainstorm good questions.

Patricia Sivori, a teacher from Paterson, New Jersey, with whom I worked for a year, had her young students think together about the topic of pets before anyone shared about his or her pet. "What kinds of things do we want to know about people's dogs and cats and fish and hamsters?" she asked. Pat used photographs of animals to help the children think concretely about what they wanted to know. The children came up with ideas, which she wrote down on a big chart:

- What colors are they?

- What do they look like?

- What do they eat?

- What do you do to take care of them?

- What are their names, and why did you name them that?

- Did your pet ever do anything bad? Tell us about it.

On the first day I visited this class, they were ready for the first pet share at their morning gathering. At that time I knew nothing about all the preparation they had done and was astounded at the richness of the storytelling that emerged. Structuring their preparation around the principles of good storytelling resulted in interesting narratives, and the audience needed no reminders about active listening.

Here are some great topics for sharing at all grade levels:

- Pets

- Stories about getting hurt or sick

- A time I got in trouble

- My cousin (not my brother or sister—those stories are mostly about conflict)

- Something I or a family member made by hand (best with a short demonstration)

- My grandma or grandpa (best if the subject comes to school)

- A time when I was scared, nervous, excited, brave, etc.

- My favorite place to be

The list will get very long if you and the children brainstorm stories you would really like to hear about. Interesting questions and friendly comments from the audience can be rehearsed ahead of time for each topic: *What are some questions we might ask the people who are sharing a story about a cousin so that we'll find out lots of interesting things?*

Using theater in your everyday classroom has the same impact as integrating any arts media—it empowers children and can bring history, science, math, and literature to life. For students whose strength is in speaking or moving, for example, storytelling might provide an easy entry into reading and writing. Give theater a chance, and watch the children talk their way into learning!

CHAPTER 7

Getting Comfortable with Poetry

When I'm by myself
And close my eyes
I'm a book getting read to a child
I'm a garden waking up
I'm a dream in someone's head
I'm an eagle in the wild
I'm a shape having fun
I'm a hand helping you
And when I open my eyes
I feel happy

—First grader

I carry inside me a TV which is on all the time
        my Aunt's horses
            a polar bear,
                some meatballs,
                    the earth, which carries us.

—Fourth grader

Both of these poems were written in response to an assignment to write an autobiographical poem using a teacher-determined starting line. Vivid and honest, they demonstrate children's capacity to imagine startling and beautiful connections. That capacity lives in all of us and is the source not only of poetry, but of new ideas and creative solutions in general.

Students benefit from learning basic poetry-writing skills, just as they benefit from learning basic drawing or movement or singing skills. And when given both a guiding structure and the freedom to surprise you, children can learn how to use language playfully and powerfully, how to create rhythm, how to choose interesting details that make their subject come alive, and how to express facts and ideas flavored by personal response.

I focus on poetry rather than other genres such as fiction and nonfiction because with poetry, the children are less likely to try to imitate popular media stories. It is easier to avoid endless replays of Walt Disney mermaids, unicorns, adventurers, and action figure heroes when you switch into an entirely different mode of writing.

What comes out is rough and minimal at first, but it is often bare-bones honest and sometimes, even at the beginning, intense and memorable. It leads to lively, perceptive writing in other genres and curiosity about the world as seen with fresh eyes. It becomes a basic tool of learning.

Lesson Structure

Learning to write poetry is a bit like learning to dance. A young child just moves—for pleasure, to express feelings, to play. Then the child moves to music and adds the enjoyment of rhythm to the pleasure of self-expression. Finally, the child might learn some steps—a structured dance with a more polished, if less spontaneous, form.

It's the same with poetry. First we invite children to say what they need or want to say, giving just a little structure—an idea, a few words to play off, a topic, or word limits. We make it as easy as possible to get the flow going. Then, after they have begun to speak from the heart about what they know, see, and feel, we introduce more organized forms to provide some architecture for their language.

No matter what the stage or content of the poetry lesson, the format I use is roughly the same each time:

Spark

Warm up student imaginations and verbal thinking with a brief chance to dream, imagine, remember, and think in an offbeat way. You might tell a story or joke, ask questions about their lives and feelings, or say or do something surprising: *I woke up this morning and was very crabby! Have you ever felt crabby, and you didn't even know why?*

Lesson topic

Describe what they will do, and read some examples of poems that use the approach or form you are asking them to use (for example, concrete imagery or a repeating line). Try out the approach or form yourself the night before, and read them that effort (as you wrote it and not polished).

Work

Give students ten to fifteen minutes to write. During that time, circulate and help anyone who wants some input. I look for some interesting poems while I circulate. If I find a finished or almost finished poem that might inspire others, I interrupt the children's writing for a moment and read the poem to the class. I read it with style and enthusiasm, and it inspires others to work with more energy on their own poems.

Sharing

Collect all the poems and read some aloud. Here is where I depart from my usual policy to have children read or show their own work. I don't want any lack of *reading* skill to hamper appreciation for the good qualities in their *writing*. I prefer to read their poems back to them with emotion, rhythm, and style, so that they hear them at their most dynamic. When the young poets like what they hear, when their words sound good to them, they are inspired. Especially for new poets, I want them to know that their voices tell us true things, are funny, surprise us, and can soar! I've watched many a nonwriter get hooked at just that point. When they have written several poems and done some editing, when they can do more justice to their poetic imaginations, they will read their own poems and enjoy the appreciation of an audience. At first, however, I want them just to listen to the power of their own language.

In this chapter and in Chapters 9–13, I give examples of this format in action.

The importance of teacher response

Children need to hear how good their work is. So, I show my pleasure in their poetry. I mention something that surprises me. I laugh out loud at something that tickles me. I repeat a line with a strong rhythm so everyone can hear it again. I point to a word and describe its effect on me. I look for the poetic characteristics in which children naturally excel:

Concreteness—they are closely in touch with the details of the world around them.

Economy—they say it and stop.

Energy—eau d'exuberance is their perfume, surprise their spice.

Patterns—they see verse forms as interesting puzzles.

Metaphor—they are not afraid to lay improbable comparisons at your feet.

Rhythm—they are in tune with natural speech patterns.

Authenticity—they are more likely than not to tell the truth.

My purpose is to make a public response to language and ideas that have these qualities, and I find that there is almost always at least one thing concrete, rhythmic, terse, energetic, or authentic in everything children write.

As Sheryl Noethe says:

Your job as a teacher is to tell every student what is right about his or her work….When you point out to your students where they are at their best in their work—the funniest or the most imaginative or the truest to their vision—you give them success and they in return give you their trust. They write in the only way beautiful things are created—from the heart, without censorship or fear. That's when you get the poetry. (Collom and Noethe 1994, xvi)

In the following exercises for getting comfortable with writing poetry, I include sample teacher language to give you ideas about how to show your appreciation using specific and encouraging language rather than general praise.

Exercises to Develop Skill and Comfort with Poetry

Paying attention to details: place poems

Poets use lively, concrete details to communicate thoughts, which is something we'd like our students to do in all their writing. So begin by focusing on detailed, sensory images: What does this person, place, object look like? Smell like? Sound like? Feel like when you touch it? For example, you can ask students to write poems about places they know.

Spark

It's best if students can actually "visit" the place they are going to write about shortly before (or even while) they write about it. A picture can help. A look out the classroom window might work for a poem about the school neighborhood. To spark some concrete writing, I invited third graders in a reading intervention program to walk outside the school with me and look at the trees and shrubs, listen to the birds, watch the people go by for a few minutes. The fresher the observation, usually the more detailed the description in the poem.

You could also invite students to think about places that are special to them. They know them well, have feelings connected to them, and can call them up visually and emotionally in their minds. A guided visualization may help:

> *Close your eyes and think about one of your favorite places to be:*
>
> *Where are you standing or sitting?*
>
> *What sounds do you hear?*
>
> *What do you see?*
>
> *What smells are there?*
>
> *Reach out to touch something—what does it feel like?*

Lesson

The task is to write a poem that uses sensory details to tell the reader something about the places the students visited. After the guided visualization, for example, you might ask students to put into words what they just experienced in their minds: *Christina, tell us about your place, and I'll write down the details on this chart.* Make a list of the words she uses to describe her place. If necessary, prompt her: *Did you touch the water in the lake? What did it feel like? Was it cold or warm?* The list of words and phrases becomes a vivid little poem that you can all then read together.

Or you might read aloud a poem that uses sensory details to describe places. (See the Resources section for anthologies of poetry.) If you wrote a poem the night before as part of preparing for the lesson, read it to the children after first telling them about the place you are describing. Tell them why you picked certain words. Ask them if you used enough detail so that they can "see" your place. It's like a game: can you give enough concrete detail so everyone can see what you saw? That will be their goal in writing these poems.

With the third graders from the reading intervention program, I provided a structure. First, I asked them to write down all the details they remembered. Next, they chose one of three words that I gave them—"looking," "listening," or "smelling"—which they could repeat in the poem to give it some shape and rhythm.

One third grader wrote:

The Summer
Looking for
   the tulips
     and bees
       wasps
         and birds singing
Looking for
   the rabbits
Looking for
   grass
     and the sun
     and
Looking at the
   doves.

Teacher response can be about the impact on the reader of the use of detail: *Your naming of specific plants and animals helps me see them in my mind.*

Writing in a structured brief form: the lune

One of the best things about poems is that they can be very short. Children who have never written much see that they can make their mark with just a few lines—and they love it! For the verbose writers, the ones who pile on adjectives and go for quantity, structured brief forms help tighten up language.

The lune is one of my favorite forms for beginning writers. A lune is a three line poem that contains only eleven words: three words in the first line, five words in the second line, and three words in the third line.

Spark

You can begin by naming an interesting topic (a time when someone was kind to you, a time when you were hurt, a description of your favorite animal) and ask a volunteer or two to tell about such a time.

Lesson

Once their imaginations are stimulated on the topic, students can freewrite for a few minutes, using specific language to describe the details about the subject. (Keep reminding your writers that details, not generalizations, are the important thing in poetry.)

The task is to write a lune about the subject of their freewriting. First describe the lune form and diagram it with word blanks:

　　____ ____ ____

　　____ ____ ____ ____ ____

　　____ ____ ____

Read an example of a lune that you have written large on chart paper or the board. Together you and the children can count the words in each line to see that the poem fits the form.

Then children review their freewriting and write a lune about the subject. A sixth grader first writes about feeling left out:

> Once I felt I was being excluded when I saw my best friend playing with someone who hates me. I wanted to ask to play, but I knew she'd say no, so I watched them walk away.

Her lune is:

> I was dumb.
> Why didn't I ask her?
> Now I'm alone.

The teacher response might note the tone and the surprise in the poem: *The disgusted tone of lines one and two turn into the sadness of line three—you wake me up with that unexpected sad voice.*

Talking to or for a subject

One of the ways that students might use poetry to learn content is to write a poem from the point of view of someone—or something—they're studying. Trying to get inside another's experience is one way to solidify learning. A "talking to or for" poem helps children practice the skills of empathy and imagination.

Spark

Bring in photographs (for example, postcards and calendar pages) or drawings of people, animals, or places. Ask the children to choose a picture they are drawn to and to simply look at it for a few minutes. Ask them to imagine what the subject of their photo or drawing might say if it could speak. To prepare for a lesson I did with a fifth grade class, I looked at the photograph on my desk of two of my grandchildren, ages four and two, dressed warmly on a cold day and staring right at me to make sure what I say about children is true!

Lesson

The task is to write a poem that "talks to or for" the subject of each child's drawing or photo. I might begin the lesson with a fifth grade class by reading the poem I wrote after looking at the picture of my granddaughters:

> Little birds
> I won't disturb your
> pink and blue feathers,
> your bright mouths,
> your eyes watching.
> You lean forward
> to catch any lies,
> to keep the nest clean.

After reading your "talking to or for" poem, invite students to write their own. Coral reef islands speak for themselves in this poem:

> Island, what do you need?
> I need the sun, earth and atmosphere, no
> pollution and you.
> I need the birds to sing me to sleep, nature
> and the world.
> I need company.

You could respond to the emotion in this poem: *If I were an island, that's just what I would want most—you! What could be more alone than an island wishing for company?*

Paying attention to rhythm

Once children get the idea of lines that are shorter than sentences and sentences that can run into the next line, they begin to write the words down with some rhythm to the line, even without knowing anything about metered verse. But the rhythm falters when the adjectives pile up and ideas are stuck together in monotonous necklaces of "and's" and "so's."

To help children hear the difference between rhythmic language and stilted language, read aloud their poems, your poems, and the work of other poets. When I read the children's poetry, I sometimes skip the extraneous transition words so the writers can hear the rhythm of short, punchy sentences mixed in with longer, thoughtful musings. When I read other poets' work, I make sure to choose poetry with highly rhythmic lines.

Rhythm through repetition

One way to help beginning writers provide rhythm in their poetry is to use a repeating line, phrase, or word.

Spark

I've done a lot of writing with children around the theme of exclusion. We talk about it a little, and I often tell a story about myself being excluded from an activity and how I felt. A personal story about the topic of a poem is a good spark because it helps bring emotion into the writing. You can ask the children if such a thing ever happened to them and how they felt.

Lesson

Then I ask them to brainstorm things that a person who was excluded might say or ask. They give me phrases such as: "Why don't you like me?" "What's wrong with me?" "Left out!" "All alone. I'm lonely." You can use any theme. For example you might ask the children, "What are some things you might say about or to someone you really care about?" Students might answer, "He makes me feel good" or "My family's my home."

Once you have collected some key phrases, you can invite students to write a poem using repetition to give some rhythm. Suggest that they begin and maybe end their poem with one of the phrases the group suggested or make up another that they like better. They might also repeat the phrase in the body of the poem. Here is an eighth grader's poem:

Alone

Alone is my companion.
An oxymoron, comfort, escape
Alone is my grandmother's companion
It shares the walls, windows and space.
When is alone a friend?
Why does he get to decide?
I sit in my closet, ten years old
Hiding from the noise and the crowd
I sit on my deck under the stars
Contemplating thoughts in my head
Grandma watches her TV show
Waiting for her visitors to come
She changes her sheets from flannel to cotton
Another quiet season for her guest room bed
When is alone a friend?
Why does he get to decide?
Why am I alone?
Why don't I be her friend?

You could comment on the effectiveness of the concrete images: *The grandmother and the boy in this poem seem to live separately in their own lonely worlds. The last line startles us into seeing other possibilities. "She changes her sheets" is a simple, concrete picture drawn for us—how sad to change your sheets eager for company, and then no one comes.*

After doing this exercise, the next time you want students to use repetition, you may not have to brainstorm first. Ask them to write a line they like or find one in their free-writing. They can use it a couple of times in the poem. That's usually all it takes, especially for older children, for repetition to become a tool in their writing.

Rhythm through everyday speech

Another way to bring rhythm—and energy—into poems is to invite students to write the way they talk. Sometimes I scribe for a student, even an older one, to allow the flow of ordinary speech to come out unharnessed to a pencil.

Spark

Begin by reading poems that incorporate real-life language. Teacher Kandace Logan and her students read *I Am From Soul Food and Harriet Tubman* by Lealonni Blake. When Kandace asked what they noticed about Blake's use of speech, the students talked about her use of slang—"sittin' on the dubs," "sittin' on 20."

"I talk that way too," Kandace said. "Not in the classroom, because not everyone might understand me. Raise your hand if you talk that way." She then asked the students to think about what they'd say in a poem that was "true to who you are—how you walk and talk, how you live your life."

Lesson

The task is to write an autobiographical poem that uses everyday speech. Kandace asked students to first make a list—to think about family, favorite memories, food, gatherings, special clothing, the neighborhood, hair styles, hang-out places. "Add to your poem things that you say and things that are special to you," she said. "Tell what is part of you in your poem." Here is a poem that not only uses everyday speech but also includes a repeating phrase:

Where I'm From

I'm from dance to the
music and smackdown with
the french braids.

I'm from get together and
have fun, a safe family is
where I'm from

I'm from "hurry up girl and
don't be late"
From a mother named Juliet saying
"don't be a know-it-all."

I'm from the smell of
candy coming from the
corner store.

> From my sister crying to
> my mother calling.
>
> I'm from the strength in the
> ring to the body on the mat.
>
> If you dug deep in my
> heart you'll find Juliet
> and Madia my golden
> Queen and Princess
> That's where I'm from.

You might respond to the energy you get from the authentic speech in the poem: *You really tell us the truth in this poem—we feel like we're in your world when you give us the language of the people around you.*

Paying attention to figurative language

The excitement of figurative language such as metaphor and simile comes from the way it bends your mind in a new direction. Of course the writer must *think* of that bend first. It calls for an ability to see things in more than one way. A fish is lightning, a streak of color, a messenger from the deep, dinner to a starving camper.

But in order for the metaphor or simile to work, the two things have to be just the right distance apart. It's like an electric charge. If the electrodes are too far apart (roses are like refrigerators holding food), no jump in understanding happens, but if they're too close (roses are like tulips—they come in many colors), you get a short circuit.

To help children learn about using figurative language, you might begin with some quick word games. For example, give students cards on which they write nouns randomly. Put the cards in a box, pull out any two of them, and together try to figure out how they are the same. Or have the students exchange cards and the second person writes a word that is related to the first, or seems funny next to the first, or is completely unrelated. Read the word pairs aloud just to see what images come up. Word play such as this will strengthen children's ability to make connections, increase their vocabularies, and make working with language the lively adventure it needs to be to spark young writers.

Metaphor through "mix and match" poems

This exercise was inspired by poet Michael Dennis Browne, who was a visiting poet at Prairie Creek School in Minnesota. He helped children create some interesting associations by asking them to write poems about an animal or an object, then chop the lines in half and mix them up.

Spark

The spark for this exercise can be a guided visualization. Ask children to close their eyes and imagine themselves as a mouse or a typewriter—any animal or thing. Stimulate their imagistic thinking and willingness to play a little with the world by having them visualize the animal or thing doing something—moving, being used, going quickly or slowly, etc.

Lesson

Then the children brainstorm a list of nouns (house, cat, baby) and think of verb phrases that describe each noun: What is that animal or thing doing? Falling down? Looking for food? Smiling? They shape the list into a "sensible" poem where each line follows this format:

I am a [noun], [what that noun is doing].

Here are a few lines from one child's initial poem:

I am a dog cowering.
I am a snowflake falling from the sky.
I am a book written deliciously well.

Alternatively, the children could make a list of the beginnings of each line—"I am a table," "I am a rooster"—and *then* add the actions to each object or animal.

Next, ask children to literally cut the poem apart line by line and then to cut each line in half after the noun. They should end up with two piles: one pile of "I am a [noun]" sections and one of the modifying phrases. Ask them to shuffle each pile and then, starting from the top of each pile, paste new lines together on a piece of paper. Here is the poem that resulted from chopping the entire list that I sampled above:

I am a mouse cowering.
I am a snowflake left in the cold.
I am a dog falling from the sky.
I am a book waiting for spring.
I am a bare tree written deliciously well.
I am a sun dog blossoming beautifully.
I am a plant caused by the cold.

You might respond to the new meanings that emerge magically from the scrambled phrases: *It's true if you turn things a quarter turn, or look at them out of the corner of your eye, that books might wait for spring and sun dogs might blossom.*

Metaphor through animal alliteration poems

A playful assignment using alliteration also helps children think in new ways.

Spark

The spark for this exercise could come from reading any book or poem, or telling a story about an animal, especially a story with interesting descriptions of the animal. Then you might ask the children to tell something special about a favorite animal. You can get them started by sharing something yourself: *The thing I notice about cats is that they often move very carefully.*

Lesson

With the children's help, create a list of animals. Next, create a list of words that could be associated with each animal, being sure that each word begins with the same letter as the word for that animal (for example, for "dog" you might list "determination"). The list of associated describing words could be made by each child individually, or you could keep going with a class list and finish the demonstration with a class poem, before asking each child to try writing a poem.

The format you use for each line of the poem turns ordinary observations about animals into playful metaphors:

I am the [describing word] in a [animal].

The words that go in each blank must start with the same letter. Each writer picks animals he wishes to use to describe himself (from the list or ones he thinks of by himself). He writes the names of the animals in the second blank of each line. He then looks at the descriptive words, or makes some up, and chooses a word to put in the first blank of the first line, being sure the word starts with the same letter as the animal, and continues filling in the blanks until the poem is complete.

Here's an example:

I am the fierce in a fox
I am the breath of a bobcat
I am the jump in a jaguar
I am the run in a rabbit
I am the try of a tiger.

You could respond to the energy and the surprise in this poem: *I picture the hot, racing bobcat, the jumping and running jaguar and rabbit, and then I hit the word "try." What is the "try of a tiger"? My mind gets all riled up and I'm excited by the surprising choice of word!*

These exercises—in which children take lighthearted liberties with language and brainstorm connections—are a beginning. The resulting poems will have metaphors that force everyone to stretch and will begin the process of writing—and thinking—nimbly.

Read Poetry with the Children

Throughout these exercises I've often suggested that you read examples of good poems by other writers. Reading good poems is a great way to cultivate an appreciation for poetic language and spirit. Whenever you get a chance, even if it's not part of a specific poetry-writing lesson, you and the children can read some poems. Read to them shorter poems or parts of poems from great writers. Read poems by other children. Read poems that are collected as illustrations in the poetry-writing books (many of those poems are by children, too). See the Resources section for a list of collections. Poets-in-residence also can help children appreciate poetry by giving students something new and fresh to aim for.

And read *your* poems aloud. Try an approach to writing poetry yourself before you give students the assignment, or write along with them. Write about what interests you; feel free to express your own ideas and feelings. Your students will come to know you better, and you, like all of us, will be nourished by self-expression. Read your efforts to them (the ones that aren't too personal)—unedited, just as you read theirs. Work on your poems, and share frustrations and breakthroughs in finding just the right word or image for a poem. Accompany them on the poetic adventure.

A CAUTION ABOUT RHYMING POETRY

When I ask children to tell me what makes a poem, the answer is inevitably, "It rhymes!" Children love to rhyme but in their attempts to choose rhyming words, the honesty and precision of their poetry can suffer. For example, a young girl wrote:

> Here is a bunny.
>
> It is very funny.

The thing about bunnies is that they are cute and soft, quick-moving, nervous, and intense, but not really funny, except in cartoons. But *funny* rhymed, and so with no more thought about the reality of bunnies, she chose *funny,* and was done with it. That's not the kind of writing that children are proud of. At best it gets a giggle for the rhyme.

Rhyming is fine for teaching word families with emerging readers. It's great in chants and class choral readings because it helps children remember language and begins their sight-word vocabulary. But when children write poetry, I eliminate rhyming at all grade levels until we get to playing with verse forms that rhyme, and that doesn't happen until I can see that they have begun to find their poetic voices.

To write a long poem about the tree of life, a fourth grader
used the pantoum form he had just learned.

Dancing without Moving

Denise Levertov, in her poem *The Communion,* describes the poet as one who "dances without moving." (Levertov 1958, 30) Writing poetry gives even the generally unsuccessful student a chance to dance with ideas and language. Maybe we've got it backwards. We teach children grammar, spelling, punctuation, sentence structure, paragraphing, transitions, and research writing first, and then, like a dessert at the end of the meal, if there is time, poetry. Maybe poetry can make it all worthwhile in the first place, can turn children on to the joy of authentic self-expression through words. After they've tasted the sweetness of "writing because you have something to say," we can take them anywhere. We might start getting research papers that are more than downloaded information. We might even get writing across the curriculum that incorporates the lively, intense, imaginative language we (and they) have come to love in their poems.

Works Cited

Collom, Jack and Sheryl Noethe. 1994. *Poetry Everywhere.* New York: Teachers & Writers Collaborative.

Levertov, Denise. 1958. "The Communion." *With Eyes at the Back of Our Heads.* NY: New Directions.

CHAPTER 8

Introduction to Planning the Arts-Integrated Lesson

Like most teachers, when I'm planning a lesson, my goal is for the learners to be fully engaged in whatever topic I'm offering to them. What I've noticed is that students are really interested when I find a way to combine drawing or singing or storytelling with reading or math or social studies. So over the years, I've figured out ways to add the arts to content area lessons as often as possible. I use a simple structure with three basic places for arts integration. What follows is a brief description of that structure, and then chapters on teaching in five content areas—reading, writing, social studies, science, and math—with the spice of the arts to whet the appetites of the learners.

Planning the Arts-Integrated Lesson

In any curriculum area, there are three primary places where we may choose to infuse the energy of the arts into a lesson:

Spark

To stimulate interest and invite children to learn, begin with a moment of imagination— a song, a quick drawing, a poem read aloud.

Work

To learn facts, discuss concepts, and develop skills in the content area, offer students some arts-inclusive choices that grab their interest, fit their varied skills and learning styles, invite self-expression, and are open-ended enough to allow for exploration, experimentation, and rich dialogue.

Sharing and Reflection

To share, display, perform, and/or reflect on work in a way that demonstrates understanding and academic growth and allows for a personal response, students can choose from a range of arts and other choices.

With this structure you are basically asking five questions:

1. What do I want the children to learn?

2. How can I use the arts to stimulate their interest, imagination, and curiosity?

3. How can I use the arts to help all the children achieve the lesson goals?

4. What kind of planning do I and the children need to do?

5. What opportunities will students have to reflect on and share their learning?

In an actual lesson, the lines between the three elements may blur. For example, we might need to repeatedly spark interest in a project that extends over a long period. Or a demonstration or performance of student work might be used to spark the next lesson.

Visual organizer for an arts-integrated lesson

A detailed lesson plan format such as the following visual organizer is a useful tool for planning an arts-integrated lesson. You might use this organizer for a while, until it becomes automatic to provide opportunities for children to make choices, engage in imaginative exploration, and share with an audience and reflect on their work.

The lesson planner on the next page includes questions that point to the purpose of each section of the plan. On the page following that, you'll find a blank organizer that you can photocopy and use for your own planning. And in each of the content area chapters, I include a sample lesson plan.

ARTS-INTEGRATED LESSON FORMAT

LESSON TOPIC:_____

Goals | *What concepts, skills, and/or information do I want children to learn?*

Spark | *How can I begin this lesson so that I engage all the students and get them thinking about the concepts, facts, and skills I want them to learn? What will I do to heighten their personal connection to the topic?*

Group Inquiry | *What information, resources, or skills do students need in order to complete this lesson? How much instruction do they need before they can do the work required by this lesson? What prior learning do they need to draw on?*

Choices | *In what ways can students practice the skills or learn the information targeted in this lesson? How might they show their understanding of the topic? Do I have the necessary materials for the choices I am thinking about or that students might come up with?*

Planning | *Will I have students make a written planning sheet or will I have a conversation with them? What questions do I need to ask to help them clarify their plans? Are there students for whom I will limit choices?*

Work | *How will I group students? Which choices will probably need the most attention from me? What questions might I ask to keep students focused on the goals of the lesson? What questions might I ask to stimulate extensions of the lessons for students who "finish" early or who need/want the excitement of further exploration?*

Reflection and Sharing | *How much time do we have for sharing the results of our work? Who will share? When else might we have additional sharing for this topic? Will I use a results sheet or other written reflection?*

Use of side circles: The circles on the right are reminders. They provide a place to note the art forms you might use to teach at different points in the lesson. You can see at a glance what art forms you have (or have not) included and where.

BLANK ARTS-INTEGRATED LESSON FORMAT

LESSON TOPIC: _____

Goals

Spark

Group Inquiry

Choices

Planning

Work

Reflection and Sharing

CHAPTER 9

Using the Arts to Teach Reading

As an English teacher, I considered myself successful when my students responded to a piece of literature on an emotional as well as a rational level, because I knew that their emotional response would keep them involved in language in a way that no grade incentives or literal understanding could match.

Students need to decode words with enough fluency to maintain interest, and they need to understand the literal meaning of what they read—teaching them these skills is definitely part of our job. But we also want to help them respond to language on an emotional level, to feel its beauty and power. We want them to smile and laugh and get indignant and curious and confused and excited. By inviting these personal connections, the arts will:

- Arouse interest in language and amuse us

- Build vocabulary

- Deepen comprehension

- Build phonemic awareness and pronunciation skills

Poetry

Reading poetry aloud is probably my favorite way to arouse interest in language. I know that if I can capture students' imagination and interest them in the rhythmic sounds and vivid imagery of poetic language, then I have focused them (many for the first time) on the amazing possibilities of language. Think of all the poems you know that ring with sound, surprise you, or touch you with their tender imagery.

When I read poetry to students, I sometimes repeat a phrase or word—stop in the middle of a line and say, "I've got to say that again!" They hear my involvement as a reader, as well as the writer's passion. This repetition is enough, in some cases, to arouse student interest in the sounds of words as they combine and recombine to make meaning.

Kandace Logan, who teaches a poetry unit every year with her fifth graders, says that poetry is the key that unlocks the prison of low confidence with language. I participated one day when Kandace introduced the poem *I Am From Soul Food and Harriet Tubman* by Lealonni Blake. (Christensen 2000, 20) The poem opened up a discussion of slang: they "bout to bounce to the store," and wondering "Wassup?" Some students heard, perhaps for the first time, the words of their home and neighborhood used in their classroom.

Kandace and her students were immersed in a study of language, its meaning, derivations, variations, and color. More than that, the students were awake and alive, interested in language. And if they experience such moments repeatedly during their school lives, maybe they will become hooked on language—what it tells us, what its subtlety suggests, what it makes us feel.

Theater

Theater, too, can help capture children's attention. In addition, theater can help children understand narrative structure, build crucial skills in vocabulary and sentence structure, and deepen comprehension.

Storytelling

Say, "Let me tell you a story," and watch children's eyes light up. From a toddler's fascination with changes in voice and expression to a six-year-old's entranced following of the story moment by moment, to the thirteen-year-old's escape from the day's problems into the adventures of an exciting plot and a hero with whom to identify, young people seem to love to hear and see stories told. And while they're listening, they're also learning because storytelling leads to a high level of participatory listening—the kind of listening you do in a conversation when you know that after the speaker stops, it will be your turn to come up with a response or a new idea for consideration.

Using storytelling to understand narrative structure

I come to the end of a story I've been telling my granddaughters:

> "Apple the tailor was admired for his fine and ingenious sewing, but mostly people loved him because he was a...." I pause, and my granddaughters call out, "mensch!!"

> "And so the day of the picnic came," I continue. "It was sunny and the grass was dry and soft. Everyone gathered on the town green. They all grabbed onto the edge of the huge tablecloth, turned their backs on the center, and walked until they felt the tug of

the unfurled cloth. Then they turned and gasped—before them was the biggest, most beautiful tablecloth any of them had ever seen. 'This is perfect, Apple,' they cried. 'It will hold us all!' So for the first time ever, all the people of Minsk were able to sit together for the spring picnic."

My granddaughters smile a little and nod their heads. I can tell by their body language that they know the story is coming to an end and they are getting ready to say "Goodbye for now" to characters who have completely engaged their interest for ten, twenty minutes, maybe longer. How do they know? They hear events getting resolved. They sense that the characters are somehow working things out or letting things go. Storytelling has helped them understand narrative rhythm.

Books have stories, too, but there is something about a told story that frees listeners to ask questions and imagine other possibilities or elaborations on the basic story. And when children are the storytellers, particularly when they retell stories from written literature, they learn to identify and use narrative structure and understand content more deeply.

Here are some participatory storytelling activities that can help children understand basic narrative structures:

• Interrupt your story to ask for predictions of what will happen.

• Ask the children to add an episode in a round robin story.

• Create a character and invite the students to tell stories about him/her.

• Tell a story with a variety of endings and have the children pick their favorite.

• Have the children suggest ways to tell the story from different characters' points of view.

Using storytelling to build vocabulary

In addition to capturing children's attention, teaching them about narrative structure, and honing their listening skills, storytelling also helps children build vocabulary.

Putting new words into sentences is a standard way to learn vocabulary. But putting those sentences together to make a story makes the whole thing colorful, sometimes playful and funny, and therefore, memorable. For example, if a vocabulary list includes "dirigible," "elevation," "reptile," "engineer," "hors d'oeuvres," "horizon," and "accelerate," the students and I might include the words in a group story:

> Dan, the engineer, wanted to launch his dirigible so that he could see from a high elevation. He had trouble getting it started, but then it began to accelerate. Pretty soon he could see on the far horizon a giant reptile about to eat a crab for an hors d'oeuvre. "Wow," Dan exclaimed, "I think I've gone too far with this thing!" and he headed for home.

What will the storytelling accomplish that flashcards or individual sentences wouldn't? A laugh. A light moment shared in community. A memory of the incident and probably of most of the words along with it.

Simulated interviews

Simulated interviews are an effective way to dramatize characters and develop the capacity to understand character motivation. Appropriate for every grade level, simulated interviews can occur simply and spontaneously as part of discussing a piece of literature. A student responds to interview questions, representing the feelings, desires, or experiences of a character. For example, after reading Patricia Polacco's *Chicken Sunday,* you might ask:

> *Who wants to be Mr. Kodinski? All right, here are the questions for you. Mr. Kodinski, why were you so angry at the children?*
>
> Mr. Kodinski: *I thought they had thrown eggs at my door.*
>
> *Why did you decide to help them?*
>
> Mr. Kodinski: *I loved their pretty eggs. They reminded me of the eggs people used to make in the old country.*

Although students answer in the first person, as though they were the character, I recommend that students use their own accents and speech patterns rather than attempting to imitate the character's speech because those imitations can easily—and unintentionally—turn into parodies. As questions are asked and answered, the story slowly emerges, as does some of the motivation for the characters' actions and their feelings. The rest of the class listens, not the way they listen to recitations of right answers, but the way they attend a play.

Pantomime

In pantomimes, children express the actions described while the story—fact or fiction—is told or read. Fairy tales or contemporary stories come alive with a visual portrayal. Marilyn Kammueller, a kindergarten teacher in St. Paul, does *The Mitten* by Jan Brett with her students. The children play the grandmother (Baba), the boy (Nicki), and the animals who crawl, one by one, into Nicki's mitten: the mole, rabbit, hedgehog, owl, badger, fox, bear, and finally the mouse! The children crouch low, pretending to be inside an expanding mitten, until bam! The mouse tickles the bear who sneezes so hard that everyone tumbles out, eight children scooting across the classroom. It is the highlight of the story, of course, and it's unlikely that any of them will forget it.

Music

Music can play an important role in helping children learn to read. Singing songs can increase reading fluency, build phonemic awareness, and help children learn to spell. And music added to stories can enhance understanding and connection to the text for readers of all ages.

Using songs with early readers

Many primary teachers write songs on large charts and invite children to sing along as a way to help children build phonemic awareness, pronunciation skills, fluency of speech, and decoding. The melody itself seems to move them from word to word. The children memorize the words of the song, along with the melody, and "read" those words on the chart as they are singing. This gives them the confidence that comes from the words rolling out fluently, just like real reading! As kindergarten and first grade teachers well know, this memorized reading is an effective preliminary step for emerging readers.

So accumulate songs that everyone can sing together, write them on song charts, and make them accessible to children. Some teachers hang them on a hanger rack; others write them on extra-large paper and bind them into a big book. The book becomes a silent reading favorite for the children—a book they can sing/read on their own. A child who has begun to recognize the words in print can guide the class during the singing of one of these songs, moving the pointer along the line as the class reads/sings the song together.

Using songs to build phonemic awareness

For good phonemic awareness, children must listen carefully to the sounds made by experienced language-speakers. This tongue twisting song is great for teaching short vowels:

> Betty Botter bought some butter
> But she said this butter's bitter!
> If I put it in my batter
> It will make my batter bitter.
> So she bought some better butter
> Put it in her bitter batter
> And it made her batter better.
> So it was better Betty Botter
> Bought a bit of better butter.

From this foolishness, children accomplish three things: 1) they hear and learn to pronounce subtle differences in vowel sounds; 2) they learn to spell those differences accurately; 3) they laugh, but usually manage to get through the tongue twister anyway. The next time you remind someone about the sound of a short vowel, he'll probably remember Betty Botter and her bitter butter!

Tongue twisters can also teach consonants:

> Peter Piper picked a peck of pickled peppers.
> A peck of pickled peppers Peter Piper picked.
> If Peter Piper picked a peck of pickled peppers,
> Where's the peck of pickled peppers Peter Piper picked?

Who could forget the sound of "p" after learning that?

Think of the initial consonants and consonant blends practiced in this repetitive song, sung to the tune of *The Battle Hymn of the Republic*:

> One grasshopper jumped right over the other grasshopper's back
> One grasshopper jumped right over the other grasshopper's back
> One grasshopper jumped right over the other grasshopper's back
> And one grasshopper jumped right over the other grasshopper's back.
>
> [Chorus:]
> They were only playing leapfrog
> They were only playing leapfrog
> They were only playing leapfrog
> As one grasshopper jumped right over the other grasshopper's back.
>
> One pink porpoise popped his top and the other pink porpoise did not (4x)
>
> [Chorus:]
> They were only playing pop tops (3x)
> As one pink porpoise popped his top and the other pink porpoise did not.
>
> One sliced egg slipped up one side as the other sliced egg slid down (4x)
>
> [Chorus:]
> They were only playing slip slide (3x)
> As one sliced egg slipped up one side and the other sliced egg slid down.

It's all very silly, which is exactly why the children love it and remember it.

Increasing dynamic variety in speech

Some of the skills learned in singing, such as how to vary volume, pitch, and tempo, can help students increase dynamic variety in their speech. Use the following exercise as a warm-up to an oral reading lesson or as a morning meeting activity:

> With everyone seated in a circle, the leader says a word to the person to the right—for example, "hello," "rain," or "tiger." The word is passed from person to person around the circle. Each person says the word in a dramatic way—preferably a way that hasn't been said before, such as a new combination of loudness, melody, pitch (highness or lowness), and tempo (fast or slow).

This exercise raises student consciousness about the richness of oral language. As a follow-up, students can read sentences from their own writings, trying out various inflections, tempos, and dynamics to see which best carry the meaning.

Adding sounds to a story

Music can also be used to enhance and demonstrate understanding. Read a story to the class, showing the illustrations. Then go through the story looking for action places where you can add a sound enhancement such as body percussion sounds, vocalizations, and/or classroom instruments. You can use the pictures to suggest sounds, even when the words do not mention those elements (thumping feet for thunder, soft vocalizations for cows mooing and horses neighing, rhythm sticks clicking for the sound of a clock).

Ask for volunteers to suggest appropriate sounds for the actions. Then read the story again and call for the sounds you have planned. The whole class can decide whether the sound fits, and if not, try another. When the class is in agreement about the sounds that suit the action moments, you can read the story with all the sounds in place. You might even record the class "sounding" the book. Play the recording back, showing the pictures with the recording, and let the students see how well their sounds tell the story.

For example, here's an excerpt from *The Little House* by Virginia Lee Burton:

> One day the Little House was surprised *[ooooh!]* to see a horseless carriage coming down the winding country road *[chugga, chugga, chugga].* Pretty soon there were more of them on the road *[chugga, chugga, chugga chugga, chugga, chugga]*…and fewer carriages pulled by horses. *[clip clop, clip clop chugga, chugga, chugga chugga, chugga, chugga].* (Burton 1969, 14)

As an alternative, you might have partners decide on sounds to enhance different parts of the story, and then add the sounds at the right moment, so there is less for everyone to remember. With older students, partners can invent a visual reminder for the different sounds to prompt their memories.

An extemporaneous version of this exercise is to tell the children you want them to add sound effects, and then simply select someone when it's time to make a sound. The child comes up with one on the spot, and you keep on reading.

Sound carpets

Read-alouds can also be enhanced by adding "sound carpets"—a soft background sound made at the same time as the reader is reading or telling a story. Sounds carpets highlight the emotional component of a reading rather than the action. During a scary passage, the group might make ghostly "ooooh" sounds quietly during the reading. At a moment of high adventure, they may start a soft, rapid clapping in the background. At a tender or sad moment, they may add quiet humming or a soft lullaby. For the child who was listening without really hearing, the background sound makes it almost impossible to ignore the author's intent. Engagement with text at the level of exploring mood, tone, pace, and emotion creates excited, sensitive, even inspired readers.

Drawing

Drawing and reading go together naturally. Illustrating a scene from a book or drawing a favorite character is a familiar and popular way for children to demonstrate comprehension. If a student accurately portrays the details of the text, I will know that the student has read carefully and remembers what she read. For that, she needs a few drawing lessons and lots of guided practice (see Chapter 3).

It's also helpful if students have an opportunity to plan their drawings before plunging in, so that they can be clear about what they are drawing and why. There is no point, for example, in making a picture of a generic boy standing next to a generic dog to show understanding of the complexity of Marty, the main character in Phyllis Naylor's book *Shiloh*. What is the point of interest in the picture? What will the viewer learn about Marty's feelings and motivations? Pictures drawn without planning tend to be throw-away ventures.

Students usually need some structure to help plan a drawing that really does illustrate a fact or mood or idea about the subject. On the following page is a sample student planning sheet for making a visual image to illustrate a topic.

STUDENT PLANNING SHEET
FOR VISUAL IMAGES

Name _____ Date _____

Topic _____

Title of drawing _____

What will the drawing teach the viewer about the topic?

_____

How will you make this point? _____

_____

Medium _____

Materials needed _____

Due date _____

The student submits the completed planning sheet to the teacher, who may discuss the plan, make suggestions, or direct the student as necessary, before signing off on the plan. Then during the work on the drawing, and in the reflection afterwards, both learner and teacher can reflect on how well the drawing communicates its intended point.

Movement

Retelling a story or poem through movement is a good way for students to deepen their understanding of the text. Using movement is similar to using pantomime. As with pantomime, you can use movement spontaneously with the whole class any time, with little or no preparation, and imprint the plot physically in the body and minds of the movers and visually in the minds of the audience. But there's a difference in emphasis between movement and pantomime. Movement focuses on the mood and emotions of the moment through whole body action, while pantomime focuses more on facial expression and specific interactions with other people and things.

For the first experience with retelling through movement, reread the story aloud, while different children act out the events with their bodies. You can coach them as they do this. For example:

> *Show us how Little Red Riding Hood moved happily through the woods on the way to her grandmother's house.*

> *Show us how she moved as she went around the trees in the woods.*

> *Now show her as she enters the house and sees her grandmother looking so strange. She moves much more slowly now, and with a weak movement because she is a little afraid. Now she moves sideways and even backwards a few steps, because she just isn't sure about this situation.*

After the children have tried and watched a couple of retellings, it may be time for some of them to have the choice of retelling a story on their own. While other students might choose to draw a picture or use puppets to retell, partners or a small group could decide on the movements and perform the story through dance for the rest of the class. If desired, the audience might assess how the elements of movement (space, time, and energy) relate to the story or facts described and give their classmates useful feedback. For example, a child might comment, "I saw Dimitri crawling low along the ground to show the snake. Your slithery movement looked exactly like a snake!"

Using movement to understand poetry

Expressing poetry through movement is another useful exercise that takes little time. For example, ask a child to volunteer to be the cat in Carl Sandburg's poem, *The Fog,* which begins, "The fog comes in on little cat feet." Read the poem through once. Then ask the children to visualize the movement of the fog looking like a cat:

How would the "fog/cat" move? Would it be slow or fast? Would it be low or high or medium? Would the movement be smooth or choppy and angular?

Who would like to show us the fog/cat movement while I read the poem again?

What did you notice about the speed of Melissa's movement? What did you notice about the level of her body?

Melissa, why did you choose to move so slowly and keep your body so low?

The call for nuanced movement evokes a more nuanced appreciation of Sandburg's image.

A Sample Arts-Integrated Reading Lesson

So, how do we put together an arts-integrated reading lesson? Let's take a look at a sixth grade class that has just finished reading *Uncle Jed's Barbershop* by Margaree King Mitchell, which explores the themes of deprivation, discrimination, solidarity, and perseverance. The teacher wants to make sure that the children appreciate the complexities of at least one of those themes, and she decides on discrimination. She starts by telling them about a time she experienced discrimination and invites them to share their own stories.

She then gives them an opportunity to show their understanding of the theme of exclusion. First, she initiates a discussion to make sure students understand each of the important vocabulary words. She then shows them a visual image of the theme of exclusion, with the goal of sparking their thinking and clarifying instructions.

Students choose an art form to use, the teacher lets them know what art materials are available, and the children begin planning. As they plan, the teacher circulates around the room, talking with each child. When she's approved the plans, the children begin work. At the end of the work period, the children have a chance to share with each other their images, stories, songs, or movement—and through them, their thoughts and feelings. During the sharing, the teacher makes sure that they connect their work to the themes and events in the book.

Many students have chosen to make visual images so the class decides to create a display. They label each image and explain its connection to the text. For the rest of the year, long after the discussions about the book, long after the display is down, the teacher and students will remind each other of this theme, the concrete examples they drew from their own lives, and the book that sparked it all. That's what a good book means to a good reader—a permanent marker of certain valuable ideas and facts and feelings—preferably shared with others.

What I have just described is a reading comprehension lesson made more accessible and more engaging by arts-integration. Here is its plan:

LESSON TOPIC: *UNCLE JED'S BARBERSHOP*
READING COMPREHENSION (Fifth, sixth grades)

Goals

To develop the skill of identifying and developing a theme in a piece of literature; to make connections between that theme and students' lives: how discrimination has hurt them or people they know, what they or others have done to overcome the damage it does.

Spark

I tell a story about a time I was excluded—maybe about experiencing religious discrimination in college.

Storytelling

Group Inquiry

As part of understanding the themes, it's important to discuss what terms like "discrimination," "exclusion," and "perseverance" mean as they apply to the story in *Uncle Jed's Barbershop*. Additional ways to help students understand these terms include:

• Inviting students to share a time when they experienced these things

• Showing visual images that depict the experience of loneliness and hurt

• Reading some poetry about exclusion

Storytelling Visual arts Poetry

Choices

Brainstorm ways that the students can show their own experience with being excluded or discriminated against. Offer choices that include poetry, song, movement, drama, and visual arts.

Poetry Music Theater Movement Visual arts

Planning

Children choose what they want to do. Each individual fills out a planning sheet indicating choice, as well as the materials and resources needed to do the project.

Work

Sign off on planning sheets. Work with students who are stuck and help them plan. Keep these questions before them: *How did you feel? How can you show us that feeling in what you are drawing or writing or dramatizing, etc.?* Allow 40 minutes; give at least two reminders of the time to avoid last-minute panic. Students who don't finish can do so for homework.

Reflection and Sharing

Next day, review and model how to be a good peer responder (see Chapter 10). Circle up for sharing: songs, storytelling, movement, skits—20 min. to share (one student per genre). Connect the themes back to *Uncle Jed's Barbershop: How did the author and illustrator show the feelings of the people in the book?*

Storytelling Music Theater Movement Poetry Visual arts

In this lesson, students had a lot of choices and an opportunity to work with a range of art forms to connect a powerful text to their own lives. But we could also elicit strong text-to-self connections with perhaps only two or three choices. Throughout this book, you'll see descriptions of lessons; some are quite elaborate, offering lots of choices for student expression, and others are quite simple, with all students working in the same art form. Begin at a level where you're comfortable and the children have sufficient experience, and build from there.

WORKS CITED

Burton, Virginia Lee. 1969. *The Little House*. Boston: Houghton Mifflin.

Christensen, Linda. 2000. *Reading, Writing, and Rising Up: Teaching About Social Justice and the Power of the Written Word*. Milwaukee, WI: Rethinking Schools Ltd.

CHAPTER 10

Using the Arts to Teach Writing

Teacher and writer Vivian Paley is a master at the technique of having young children tell a story to her while she writes it down. Then, while she reads the story to the group, the author (and friends) act it out. "There is no preparation or lines to learn; one simply follows a narration that sounds like any child's ordinary speech. No wonder those in the audience are willing to accept almost any sort of role, one by one, around the rug. It is as natural as play itself and all are given a fair chance to be in the spotlight." (Paley 1999, 90–91)

The stories come from the children's lives and imaginations. In the telling and in the later acting out, they are expressing themselves as they choose. The story is truly theirs. Lucy Calkins quotes a child who tells her, "Nobody can tell you how to write your piece. You're the mother of your story." (Calkins 1986, 6)

Giving birth to stories is the beginning of writing for the lucky children Paley teaches. At an early age, they have begun to think of themselves as competent storytellers and writers. If they have continuing opportunities to communicate effectively through words, in the third and fourth grades they might be the class playwright, and they might learn sentence structure, grammar, and punctuation as a natural extension of their desire to communicate their thoughts and feelings to an audience. Poetry, music, theater, drawing, and movement can all play a role in bringing children to writing. In this chapter you'll see examples of using the arts to:

- Increase children's interest in written language

- Spark ideas for writing

- Clarify thinking

- Teach grammar, vocabulary, and sentence structure

But before investigating the specific art forms, let's spend some time thinking about audience.

The Importance of Audience

Lucy Calkins says that her own writing process begins not with "jotted notes or rough drafts but rather with relationships within a community of learners." (Calkins 1986, ix) No amount of what Calkins calls "synthetic writing-stimulants" (Calkins 1986, 4) can substitute for the deep, personal involvement that comes from communicating to an attentive listener something about the way we think or feel. "Beneath layers of resistance, we have a primal need to write. We need to make our truths beautiful, and we need to say to others, 'This is me. This is my story, my life, my truth.' We need to be heard." (Calkins 1986, 5) Yes, there are times when people write passionately and powerfully in a journal seen only by their own eyes—there is fulfillment, even relief, in putting ideas and feelings on paper. But most of the time, most people want someone on the other side receiving their words.

Because audience is such an essential part of writing, it's important to pay attention to how you and the students respond to each other's writing. When I'm responding to student writing, I don't critique, particularly not in the early stages. Instead, I listen for intention, humor, surprise, style, and rhythm, and I comment on what I hear: *Chantal, the sound of all that jumble of nonsense words really made me listen. The words sound like English, but they're not. It's like a joke on the audience!*

In addition to paying attention to your own response, it's important for students to become a receptive and encouraging audience for each other's work. There are certain skills that children need to learn and practice in order to be a good audience: listening respectfully, asking good questions, and making empathic comments. To help students learn these skills, I may start by sharing a piece of my own writing. We brainstorm key questions to ask or comments to make in response to my writing: *What are some questions you can ask or comments you can make to me that would really help me with my writing?* I then extend the conversation to include their writing: *What kinds of questions and comments and suggestions would help you as a writer?*

The following list offers some ideas for responding to peers' work:

Favorite parts

My favorite part/sentence is _____ because _____.

I like the word, _____, because _____.

The dog was my favorite character in the story—he acted just like my dog does.

Plot

What will happen next?

Who is going to win the prize at the end?

Setting

Where does your story take place?

What did the woods look like after the snow fell?

I can really picture the scene where they were lost because you describe it in detail.

What did the house look like? What did her bedroom look like?

Characterization

Who is your favorite character and why?

Do you know anyone like that character? Tell us about her.

Character motivation:

• Why did the kids make fun of her?

• Why didn't he want to go home?

• What made him so afraid?

Information

What does the raccoon nest look like?

I'd like to know more about how raccoon babies learn to get their own food. Do you know anything about that?

Descriptive language

I like the colorful words you used, like _____ and _____.

Could you give us words to describe the cave? I can't picture what it looks like.

Rhythm and sentence structure

I like the way you use a bunch of short sentences in a row—it sounds peppy and alive.

I got a little mixed up in that long sentence—could you read it again?

You may decide to practice one or two "categories" of responses at a time as children are learning about them, for example: *Today we were focusing on descriptive language in our writing. So as people read, listen for words that make a picture in your mind and be ready to ask or make a comment about descriptive words.*

You can then model and practice how to ask questions about descriptive language, make respectful comments, and finally how to make helpful and courteous suggestions, when invited to do so. A few formats for teaching these skills may help:

Introduce types of questions

"How" and "why" questions usually bring out the fullest answers.

Write out questions and comments

After hearing the story, the listeners write questions and comments for the author. They either give them to the author, perhaps to get written responses, or take turns reading them to the author in the circle and getting a response.

Teach closing comments

Modeled by the teacher first, these provide closure at the end of a reading. Students can volunteer to give closing comments once they understand the structure. These closing comments usually include summary statements or a compliment or wishing the author well: "I hope you write a lot of good stories like this one this year."

After students have generated a list of good questions and comments and have developed some skill in responding, they are ready to listen actively and productively to each other.

Poetry

The other side of the writer-audience equation is that children need to write in a way that invites their audience to grab on and make personal connections to what they have heard or read. Writing poetry is a good place to begin. The rich, compressed, sensory language of poetry excites many emerging writers and their listeners. With its straight talk and permission to express feelings as well as ideas, most children seem to get hooked on poetry, especially when they get a chance to hear their words read aloud to everyone. The result is writing that has vitality, that everyone wants to hear and read.

Kandace Logan told me about several "nonwriters"—children who resisted writing and always wanted to know "How long does it have to be?"—who became some of her most eager poets. That has been my experience, too—for example, with seven-year-old Erik who was progressing pretty well in his reading, but purely hated to write. "It's too hard," he'd say. He listened while his classmates sat in Author's Chair and read long stories they were making into "books." The more they wrote, the less Erik wanted to even try. He knew that he just couldn't write, that he hated writing—until someone helped him write a four-line poem. It was one spare, packed, quirky image and everyone, especially Erik, liked it.

Kandace and I agree that it's that factor of brevity that often lures the beginners. Lunes are a type of structured, brief poem that you can teach to young writers (see Chapter 7 for more about writing lunes). Not only will they enjoy writing something that's so short, but they'll also learn to convey an idea with one sharp, clear image—an important skill in all kinds of writing.

Erik continued to write poetry and began to think of himself differently. "I'm a writer," he told me. "You know—poetry and stuff." He seemed captivated by the verbal pictures he could make in just a few lines. He loved that he was "finished" in such a short time!

Poetry also frees hesitant writers because they don't have to worry about using the correct spelling and punctuation. Kandace Logan says, "I tell them not to worry about saying things right— just get the words down." Poets are allowed to invent their own rules about a lot of things—as with the poets e e cummings and bell hooks avoiding capitalization. Punctuation is a creative act in a poem.

For the first time, perhaps, child writers can make choices about where to put periods and commas based on the *effect* they want, not just on the punctuation rule book. Poetry permits us to go back to the reason for punctuation in the first place—to help communicate our words the way we mean them, the way we wish them to be received. Chapter 7 contains more ideas on writing poetry with children.

Visual Art

Making visual images is a commonly used prelude to writing. If we want the writing to be exceptional, however, it's dangerous to merely invite students to "make a picture." They are likely to grab the nearest material (which unfortunately is usually markers) and quickly draw a stick figure or a cartoon. However, if the image they make is accurate and sensitive to the character, event, or phenomenon they wish to describe, it's much more likely that the writing will be, too. So, before using drawing as part of the writing lesson, spend some time teaching basic skills, creative use of materials, and care for materials (see Chapter 3) so that careful drawing can lead to observant descriptive writing.

You can also use other people's visual art as a spark for writing. If you want children to write about spring, let them look at drawings or photographs of spring. Invite them to use these images to stimulate their memories of spring. Visual images could also be part of an expository writing assignment. As children describe what they see, they develop the skill of accurate, descriptive reporting.

Using visual images to teach grammar

Even sentence structure can be improved through visual images. When I teach grammar, I try to give a sense of the architecture of the English language through visual symbols I make out of colored tagboard:

Blue triangles are nouns (triangles because they stay put).

Smaller purple triangles are adjectives and articles, since they relate to nouns.

Red circles are verbs (circles, because they move easily).

Smaller orange circles are adverbs, since they relate to verbs.

Small white rectangles are conjunctions.

Pink arrows are prepositions.

In the first lesson with the symbols, I lay out the most common sentence structure in English—Δ O Δ (Noun Verb Noun)—usually composed into a *Subject Verb Object* combination: *Mary pets dogs. Sam bakes cakes.* If you want to begin enhancing those bare skeleton sentences, you can add adjectives and adverbs: *Mary pets a black, frisky dog gently. Clever Sam baked a moist, sweet, chocolate cake.* Now we've got Δ O ΔΔΔΔ o for Mary's sentence, and ΔΔ O ΔΔΔΔΔ for Sam's sentence.

Students can learn about the structure of language
by manipulating paper shapes of different colors.

After a short time, students can make sentences for any combinations of symbols I give them, and diagram sentences using the symbols. While I have used this strategy with third graders, other teachers have used it with intermediate and middle school students. A middle school teacher told me that her students understood more and tested better with this visual shapes approach to grammar than with any other introduction to grammar and sentence structure she had used before.

This approach has two powerful advantages: visual imagery makes something as abstract as sentence structure more accessible, and manipulating the symbols can be playful. My students pretended to talk in triangle-circle-triangle speech, instead of the words the symbols stood for. The variations and possibilities for silliness are endless. Grammar symbols can add playfulness and invention to morning message charts, for example, and help teach writing skills during one of the most social parts of the day.

Eventually everyone shares a common vocabulary to describe sentences, a handy thing when you are trying to help a child move from short, choppy simple sentences to complex sentences that can express more complex ideas. And in teaching writing, mini-lessons using the grammar shapes can be interspersed with lots of opportunities for writing, so the children can apply their newly learned grammar skills.

Theater

Theater, especially theater with movement, is one of my favorite art forms to use with writing. Students are eager to show an event or story line with their bodies, and then they can write about it.

Pantomime

Pantomime is a great prelude to writing. A child can pantomime coming home from school, discovering nobody in the house, and eating a whole package of cookies. Then he can tell the story to a friend or to the class. Finally, after the images and maybe some dialogue with the returning mother are clear in his mind, he can write the story. The child's body as well as his mind will remember what happened because of the reenactment. He is much more likely to use just the right verbs and colorful descriptive language than if he wrote only from memory or just made something up.

Pantomime also works well as an exercise to teach the skills of accurate reporting. There are endless variations on scenes that can be acted out and then written about. To prepare for standardized tests, where a favorite question is to ask children to write instructions for a specific task, children can watch a live simulation of a person doing something step-by-step, and then write instructions. The actor then acts out the process again, and everyone can look to see what details she left out or got wrong in the written description. Accuracy becomes part of the game.

Collaborative storytelling

Storytelling connects well with writing. For example, as a warm-up for writing or as a way to practice narrative techniques such as plot sequencing and character development, students can tell stories collaboratively, sometimes using words, sometimes pantomime. Collaborative storytelling allows students to create as they go, a continuous story to which everyone contributes as little as a phrase or as much as a paragraph to move the story along.

Small groups of children decide on a story they will tell. It might be a retelling of a story they all know (for example, a fairy tale) or one they make up together. When children choose to make up a story, the teacher can give them a starting point and a structure to help shape the story:

> *Let's tell a story about a child who wakes up on a Saturday and is excited to go meet with her friends and have a fun day. Then something happens to frustrate her—something goes wrong. She has to solve this problem, and then finally gets to be with her friends. You can figure out how to show her getting up and being excited, and then what goes wrong and how she deals with it. Each group will have a chance to act out their version of the story.*

To tell the story, children can stand in a circle, shoulder to shoulder. The first child begins the story. After two or three lines, the teacher says, "Stop. Next person continue the story from there," and so on around the circle.

When the story is told through pantomime, the children take turns being the character and acting out what that character does next. The teacher translates the visible action into an oral narrative. This takes liberal translation sometimes and it's important that children understand that the narrator is also the interpreter. They may want to interrupt and say, "No. This is what I meant." For the sake of continuity and story flow, ask them to wait until later, during debriefing, to tell what they were *really* trying to show. The twists and turns the story might have taken if the teacher had interpreted the actions differently give students an appreciation for rich possibilities in any plot line.

Collaborative storytelling can take as much or as little time as is available. The teacher can end the story by inviting the next two participants to "make an ending now," or "bring it on home." Then a new story can begin, or a sequel to the one just finished, or the activity can be declared over. At this point the class may move into writing fiction—telling stories based on what the class has just contrived or making new stories. The collaborative storytelling activity opens the imagination and helps release the narrative flow.

*Fourth graders collaborate on the script for an original play
that will use puppets created from milk cartons for their characters.*

Movement

A mood for a story or topic, or sometimes whole pieces of writing, can come to would-be writers through movement. For example, in a primary grade classroom, before inviting children to write about a season, the teacher can lead a discussion and make a web or list about the associations they have with that season. Then small groups of students can take turns moving in ways that evoke some of the items on the list: birds fluttering about and nesting, and gentle rain, perhaps, for spring; swimming, playing ball, eating watermelon for summer; leaves falling and a harvest moon rising for fall; strong winds blowing and snow falling for winter. The little dances can be staged by small groups while the others watch. After these short performances, students can begin writing, choosing language that might express the season they have already explored with their bodies and imaginations.

Movement is an especially powerful antecedent to writing poetry, since the poet seeks to use rich, tangible images to convey a blend of feeling and thinking. The writing about the seasons might naturally come out as poetry after the expressive movement. A student's movements may express sadness or fear or joy, and the poetry could pick up where the dance left off.

For older children, movement can provide the spark for a writing assignment. For example, before writing an essay on interesting careers, everyone can pantomime the career topic about which she or he plans to write, and the rest of the class can try to guess the career. Or movement to the sounds of Latin American music might precede a writing assignment about a country in South America. The movement invites attention to the topic and stimulates interest in an enjoyable way.

Using movement to teach parts of speech and build vocabulary

Movement can also be used to teach parts of speech and build vocabulary at the same time. For example, to teach parts of speech the teacher might say:

> *Let's show some verbs: walking, skipping, hopping, running, crawling, bicycling, marching, etc.*

> *Let's show some nouns: house, ball, car, door, teapot, flower, tree, leaves on the ground.*

> *Now some adverbs: quickly, tenderly, excitedly, sleepily, fearfully.*

> *And adjectives: pretty, angry, busy, worried, tall, tiny, itchy, calm.*

The class does these movements as the teacher calls out the words or individuals demonstrate different words. A game version would have children demonstrating one of the words while others try to guess the word and/or part of speech. If you are learning some new vocabulary words, a list of new words posted on the wall will give clues as to which word is being represented by the movement.

Verbs are ideal for movement exploration, of course. Students' vocabulary of action words will explode if the words are made explicit through actual physical movement. You can run through groups of verbs as a game in morning meeting:

Today we'll explore actions that you can do with your face. Here is a list. We'll start by reading through the list together. Then each of us will get a word from the list, repeat the word and make that movement using our face muscles (no words or sounds). Let's all read the list together:

smile	*frown*	*sneer*	*pout*	*scowl*	*grin*
yawn	*chew*	*wince*	*grimace*	*squint*	*blink*
wink	*gape*	*stare*	*glare*	*leer*	*worry*
breathe	*blow*	*cry*	*wonder*	*droop*	*excite*

After you've read the list, you give the first word on the list to a student: *Who would like to be first? OK, Serena. First word: "smile!"* Serena repeats "smile," and then smiles.

After all students have had a chance to demonstrate an action word, you can use these words to play *Pass the Gesture.* Begin by inviting students to raise their hands if they need a reminder about the gesture that goes with a particular word. Then Serena turns to the student on her right, Leona, and smiles. Leona copies Serena's facial expression, then turns to the student on her right, Alex, and passes Alex her own facial expression for "frown." The activity continues around the circle.

For older students you can extend the game into a version of the game *Concentration:*

I'll begin with my word, "worry." I'll say it, show it, and then say and show a different action word from our list. Whoever has that word, repeats it and shows it, and then says and shows a different word. We'll start slowly, and then try to speed it up. Is there anyone who doesn't remember his or her word? Ready? "Worry." [Show a worried face.] *"Wink!"* [The person who has "wink" repeats it and winks, then says and shows another word—for example, "pout."]

Other groups of verbs can substitute for the face ones in these games. Some would work best with room to move from place to place and probably wouldn't work within a circle, but others work well sitting or standing in one place. Here are a few lists; you and the children can add many more. Try out each action so that everyone is clear about what the movements look like:

Arms and hands	Hands only	Legs and feet	Whole body
pound	open	kick	wiggle
sweep	close	stamp	stretch
slice	cut	tip-toe	fall
push	scratch	tap	shake
pull	squeeze	drag	sway
dig	knead	click	pounce
throw	snap	point	spin
catch	point	twist	dance

Watch speaking and writing vocabularies expand as children become intimately acquainted with a rich variety of action words!

Movement can even be used to practice punctuation skills. Assign parts: commas, periods, exclamation points, quotation marks, question marks. Read a paragraph, pausing for punctuation. The children fill it in as you read, with a hand or whole body position to represent that punctuation mark.

Music

Many teachers use music to spark and accompany writing work. For students with strong musical interests and abilities, the music may provide an easy slide into writing. For everyone else, the music can capture their attention and help them focus on fresh word choices as they try to describe what they hear and how it makes them feel.

Music is a particularly good partner for poetry. Children can write poetry that describes the mental images evoked by a piece of music. Or a lesson could begin with children painting to music, a frequently-used curriculum combination, followed by inviting students to write a poem that captures the mood of what they have heard and painted.

Music can also mark a transition from other work to writing and can provide an inspiring background to the writing process. You can begin by playing a recording of nature sounds (crickets, bird songs, the ocean), new-age sounds, or classical music to call the children away from cleaning up or researching or working on math problems and towards the special mindset of the writer. And once the children are writing, you can choose background music that sets the tone for a particular topic—*Swan Lake* for writing lyrical language, for example, or *The William Tell Overture* for action writing.

A Sample Arts-Integrated Writing Lesson

You can plan a writing lesson using the sample planning format introduced in Chapter 8. Here's how I might think through infusing the energy of the arts into a writing lesson:

Spark

Begin with pantomime, song, storytelling, visual image, musical recording, or movement to touch the emotions and trigger creativity.

Work

When possible, I like to give children a choice of genres that they're familiar working in, such as writing a letter, poem, or story. Before the students start to write, I ask them to sketch out their ideas—the pictures in their minds—before the images slide away. They can learn to make whole outlines for longer writing, but a quick list with a few key words is often enough for short pieces.

They may choose to "draw" their outline, showing main ideas or events in circles, for example, and then clustering their ideas in smaller circles around these as they sort the ideas into sub-categories.

Once they begin writing, I circulate, ready to coach students who are stuck. If a student is stuck, I sit close and ask questions that might elicit a colorful answer or even the telling of a story. Once the story is out, the struggle to generate a good idea is over. Sometimes I tell a quick story myself, to engage the blocked writer and prime the pump for similar experiences. Sometimes I ask the student to act out a little bit of the topic:

Show me how you sat and what you did as you watched the baseball game.

What did you do when the first long ball was hit?

What did you say when the pitcher struck out three batters in a row?

Acting out the story can release the words to tell it.

Reflection and sharing

I invite reflection by reading parts of the writing back to the writer while we sit side by side. I invite the child to listen and to think about the writing, respond to it, and maybe change or add to it:

How did that sound?

Can you think of some describing words you could add that would make the pictures clearer in the mind of the reader?

I got mixed up in this paragraph—can you tell me out-loud what you are telling the reader here?

And of course, as often as possible, I want to offer the opportunity to all the writers to read to an audience. This could happen between partners, in small groups, or with the class as a whole.

Arts-integrated writing lesson plan

Here's what a lesson on instruction-writing looks like using the visual organizer:

LESSON TOPIC:

WRITING INSTRUCTIONS (Fourth, fifth, sixth grades)

Goal | Students learn skill of describing how to do something so that someone else could follow the instructions successfully.

Spark | Pantomime making a peanut butter and jelly sandwich. Students record steps as they view them.

Theater— pantomime

Group Inquiry | Ask some open-ended questions: *How can a person help another person do something merely by using words? What would the teller or writer have to do to really help? Have you ever found directions confusing? What helps you the most when you're learning how to do something for the first time?*

Choices | Choice of genre: directions, list of steps, comic strip, book illustrated with diagrams.

Drawing

Planning | "Sketch" out ideas; write few key words to remind them of where they are going. For this short assignment, a quick list, rather than a full outline, is probably enough. Students can "draw" their outline, if they choose, showing main ideas or events in circles, and then clustering their ideas in smaller circles around these as they sort the ideas into sub-categories. (In front of the whole group, talk a student through a demonstration of listing steps using his/her own topic.)

Drawing

Work | As you circulate, ask questions. Have students tell or act out pieces of their writing. Read parts of their writing back to them, so they can respond to it and edit.

Theater— pantomime Movement

Reflection and Sharing | Provide opportunity for some writers to read to the class. Response from class members can take the form of questions, comments, or suggestions (if requested). If the topic permits, have students follow a writer's directions, using real materials, to see if the directions are clear and accurate. Writers could also pantomime directions.

Theater— pantomime

This format is much like a good writers' workshop, with the addition of theater, movement, even drawing elements to stimulate and structure the writing. To start, try injecting just one art form in just one place in the lesson, and add more as time and confidence permit. The movers and actors in your class will thank you by becoming more eager writers.

WORKS CITED

Calkins, Lucy McCormick. 1986. *The Art of Teaching Writing.* Portsmouth, NH: Heinemann.

Paley, Vivian Gussin. 1999. *The Kindness of Children.* Cambridge, MA: Harvard University Press.

CHAPTER 11

Using the Arts to Teach Social Studies

The study of society brings to life the past, present, and future of the people who inhabit planet Earth. And nothing enlivens that study better than the arts, which invite students to learn about people's patterns and preferences in a colorful and participatory way that makes the information real. By using the arts to teach social studies, we can:

- Increase students' personal connections to past and current events

- Deepen their appreciation for other people's ways and points of view

- Sharpen observation skills and improve accuracy in reporting information

- Help students learn specific skills, such as mapping

Theater

Theater techniques such as storytelling, reenactments, role plays, simulations, and fictionalized interviews and conversations help us tell the story of past and present society in a lively way that stimulates student interest. A middle school teacher I observed told me that when she switched from teaching English to social studies, she was at some loss to know what history teachers do and how they do it, until she figured out that it was all storytelling. For her the breakthrough came in her second or third year of teaching American history, by which time she could tell about the procession of events with some flow: abundant stories about what happened next and next and next. Even though in her classroom there was not a great deal of student participation in the telling, the students were engaged by her stories.

Storytelling helps keep the past alive. Even in an age where a thin disc can hold volumes and a click of the mouse can yield infinite pages of print, people persist in telling each other stories because storytelling about events and ideas and people grabs and holds our interest.

Re-creating moments in history

Telling the story of history needn't be one-sided, however. Minneapolis teacher Margaret Burke uses active re-creation to help students appreciate what life was like in an historical period. Students can look at a picture of a seventeenth century French drawing room with its period desk and writing tools and gain an intellectual understanding of what it was like to use those tools, but when they write with quills themselves and seal their letters with sealing wax, they truly understand and remember that people communicated more slowly and laboriously then. They appreciate the effort to write using cuneiforms on Mesopotamian clay tablets after they use their own tablets made with clay slabs and styluses made with meat skewers.

A child forges a meaningful connection with other times
and places by writing with pen and ink.

A simulation of life in the Middle Ages

Fifth grade St. Paul teacher Karen Randall introduced theater into a unit on the Middle Ages by having students assume the character of various tradespeople and artisans in Britain during the height of the guilds and craft societies. Students made booths for their wares and services, worked on making the belts or baskets of their trade, or called upon one another for services. They dressed the part, to some extent, and "lived" in their village for about forty-five minutes each day for a week. They had to research their trade and be able to explain their activities to those who toured the village (their parents, for example). Karen explains why she designed the unit with so much arts-integration:

> Considering people who lived long ago and far away involves an element of fantasy for many children at the elementary age-level. Their cognitive processes are still dependent on concrete experiences and their ability to understand the abstract concepts of space and time is just developing. This study thus approached the Middle Ages as a culture to explore rather than a set of historical facts to memorize. Whenever possible, …the curriculum allowed for participation and direct experience, emphasizing working with materials, field trips, and dramatics in order to bring elements of medieval life more fully to the children's understanding. (Randall 1988, introduction)

Karen's simulation took a week but some of the same advantages she describes can be accessed through briefer immersions in culture and history. For example, students can assume the role of characters in any historical story and the teacher can interview those characters to elicit the salient information about the period. As simple as the technique sounds, it has a transforming effect. The characters somehow seem real, just because they are speaking in the first person from that person's point of view.

A simulation of the Underground Railroad through interviews

In a simulation of the Underground Railroad designed by Origins, students are given a packet that contains condensed versions of the lives of about fifteen people from that time, written in their own words: transporters, runaways, returnees who came back to help others follow the drinking gourd, political and economic supporters of the Railroad, ship captains and safe house owners who sheltered the runaways. Students choose the character they want to portray, read the character's story to themselves, and then participate in a simulated interview with the teacher asking the questions.

Students respond to the interviewer in a manner as true as possible to the historical facts they have read about the actual person. They use the first person voice in the simulation ("I felt as if I had no other choice but to run"), but they take on neither the presumed speech patterns of the character, nor their gestures and style, because of our concern that attempts at imitating the accents of the characters could unintentionally result in something demeaning to the actual event and people.

Even with ordinary voices the effect is powerful. Terrance Kwame-Ross, who has led both a full scale reenactment of the Underground Railroad and the classroom simulation described above, remarked that of the two experiences he felt the interview simulation was actually more effective in helping students appreciate the phenomenal courage of those who resisted the slave system.

Simulated conversations

The possibilities for simulations are endless. In addition to having the teacher interview characters from history, two or more characters can interact. Martin Luther King, Jr., and Malcolm X can have a pretend conversation based on what the class has learned about each of these civil rights leaders. After reading a book of historical fiction such as *Sarah Plain and Tall* by Patricia McLachlan, four students can assume the roles of the father, the two children, and Sarah. The teacher can set the scene and the four can interact, trying to be true to what they know about the characters and their time and place in history, while the class watches. Then another four students can take on another scene. After a few "performances," the class can reflect on life on the east coast and on the prairie in nineteenth century America.

A good way to begin dramatizing historical or cultural events is to have a couple of students act out a scene while you tell or read about it. In effect, the words you speak direct the characters on the spot. For example, you might call up a few students to act out the arrival of immigrants at Ellis Island while you narrate:

> *OK. Celeste and Marcelle are in the big reception hall at Ellis Island. They're tired and hungry, but they wait quietly. Marcelle turns to Celeste and asks if she has a place to live.*
>
> [Pause to let her ask.]
>
> *Celeste tells her that she is going to live with her cousin in Brooklyn.*
>
> [Pause to let her speak.]
>
> *Even though the journey was so hard, they are glad to finally be in the United States. They hope their families will have a better life here. They talk about looking for work as soon as they can.*
>
> [Pause to let them talk.]

Because the heightened reality of this kind of dramatization can generate heightened emotions, you will want to make certain that all students in the classroom feel safe. As in the Underground Railroad simulation, we recommend that students not try to assume the speech and style of others. And to minimize the risk that some students will feel hurt or embarrassed, don't take on potentially volatile issues unless you are certain that the students can respectfully discuss differences of opinion, perception, and experience.

Build in time for group reflection

If you are going to dramatize a possibly controversial issue, let students know that they will have an opportunity to process the experience afterwards: *Pay attention to the feelings that come up*

for you as we do this simulation. We'll have a chance to reflect on and discuss those feelings afterwards.
And then you may decide to use any of a number of ways to structure that reflection, such as:

- Journaling

- Reflection form with questions

- Partner sharing around a topic or questions you assign

- Small group discussion with questions assigned

- Whole class discussion that begins with a question such as "What do you think the immigrants might have been feeling during this experience?" Or you could ask, "What did you think or feel as you watched/participated in the simulation?"

Using pantomime to dramatize historic moments

Another form of dramatization that does not require individual students to learn and perform individual speaking parts is to use a long poem, speech, or narrative and build a performance around the choral reading of it. Imagine how effective it would be to have a group of children reciting a Martin Luther King, Jr., speech as they pantomimed a civil rights march or a scene of citizens voting.

In any of these pantomimes, you and the students combine imagination with historic information to dramatize a powerful moment. The result, as always with theater, is the integration of emotion into learning—a dynamic combination that greatly increases remembering.

Using theater to begin or end a unit of study

Theater also makes a fine beginning or ending to a unit of historic or cultural studies. When I taught a unit on early Native American life in Minnesota, I gathered a few props like a variety of sticks, stones, and simple baskets, and invited students to imagine themselves in a wooded area with their families, but no shelter or food. What will you do to take care of yourselves? Students used the props to pantomime starting a fire, making a travois (a device with two trailing poles and a platform or net for transporting goods behind a horse), and building a shelter (miniature). As the volunteer actors came up and wrestled with the problems, the audience offered suggestions. I finished the lesson with an invitation to learn just how the tribal people, with only the natural materials around them, had managed to thrive.

When Tresi Smith, then a first/second grade teacher at Prairie Creek, wanted to culminate a month-long study of early Minnesota, she and her students dramatized a school day that might have happened in the late 1800s. They transformed their open classroom into rows of desks, wore kerchiefs, long skirts, and suspenders, used abacuses, and spoke only when asked (that was the hardest part!). They learned history through dramatized, first-hand experience— a lesson not likely to be forgotten.

Visual Arts

Visual arts can be a highly effective way for students to sharpen their observations and improve accuracy in showing what they've learned in a social studies lesson or unit. Nancy Beal, a New York City art teacher, describes art activities that follow field trips to local bakeries, fire stations, or parks. Upon their return, the class discusses what they have seen, answering questions such as: How were the cookies arranged in the case? What was on the fire truck? How can we show the park so that someone who has never been there would know what it is like?

Whatever they can recall is material for the image they will make. Beal has children create murals on large rolls of brown paper. For young children, she provides the baseline to help them organize their images. In groups of five or six they plan what they will include in their section. Sometimes they draw first and then paint. Other times they just paint. The murals, of course, go on the walls, and the class reflects on what they have shown in them. Although Beal doesn't suggest it, if accuracy of visual memory is one of the goals of the lesson, photographs or repeat visits to the place can provide a check on memory, stretching the children's efforts to remember things just as they were.

Third/fourth graders locate landmarks on a student drawn, painted,
and sculpted aerial map of the neighborhood around their school.

The arts can also be used to show what students have learned about different cultures. For example, students can make:

- Geometric designs in the style of Ghanaian and Nigerian cloths

- Mounted and framed cut paper images of life on the early plantations

- Colonial style embroideries

- Early Dutch dolls or stick puppets

- Pottery in Greek, Native American, and seventeenth century Chinese Ming traditional styles

- Middle Eastern mosaic tile murals

In all of these projects, children deepen their appreciation for both the crafts and the cultures they study. (Beal 2001, 189–208)

It is important to note that when art projects focus on the style of another time or culture, the specific images made by students need not imitate the traditional images of that culture. In Origins school residencies that focus on learning about Native American or Inuit cultures, for example, we take particular pains to encourage young artists to draw from their own lives about things that are meaningful to them, not to imitate other people's religious symbols. So, for example, if we are studying mask-making and wearing, we make masks, but use animals that are meaningful in our lives rather than copying the jaguars and snakes that bear deep religious significance for the people we are studying.

Poetry

Poetry, too, has a role in the study of society. Poetry captures life on the level we most deeply encounter it. Listening to each other's poems, children can learn first hand about each other: I like something; you don't. You talk this way; I talk that. Your family fights a lot; so does mine. I see you. You see me. It's the beginning of acceptance rooted in the realities of who we really are. It's multicultural understanding person by person, social studies from the inside out.

Kandace Logan asked her fifth graders to describe their worlds, the pieces of life they think of when asked about themselves. Patterned on the poem *I Am From Soul Food and Harriet Tubman* by Lealonni Blake (Christensen 2000, 20), the children wrote poems from their own lives and cultures, such as this one:

Where I'm From

I'm from the smell of egg rolls
crisp in and out from
the maker of my mother

I'm from cops and robbers running and chasing
each other in the night

> I'm from all the stories that my uncles and my father
> tell, to my cousin Tracy, Steve, and Pang Kou making
> jokes and acting up
>
> I am from family picnics, eating and playing games
> in the middle of May
>
> I am from "Have you done your homework" and "Stop
> running" from my dad and mom's voice.
>
> You may look in my doctors appointment records and
> you'll see that my blood matches up with my parents.
> That's where I'm from.

In addition to original poetry by the children in your class, another source for studying human society, of course, is published poetry and stories that capture other people's realities. The poetry of people from a variety of cultures offers understanding at a deep level of the similarities and differences among us. For example, hearing the poems in *Looking for Home: Women Writing About Exile* (Keenan and Lloyd 1990), we begin to appreciate what it means to be a country of immigrants, how unsettling and confusing it is to try to change your being, and how that confusion can show up in alienation from school or work, or in anger on the street.

Movement

Because movement offers an anchor to the concrete, it can help children learn about the physical geography of the world. For example, imagine you're doing a lesson on mapping and you want to teach about points on the compass:

> *Who can tell us in which direction I'm pointing? If that's north, then what is this direction, Darnel? And this direction, Elizabeth? And finally this direction, Harry? Everyone stand now, and let's see if we can agree each time on the direction I call out. Point with your right arm and hand in the direction and let your whole body lean towards the direction you are pointing. Ready? South! East! South! West! North! South! It looks beautiful—we're all flowing together, like a wave. I'm going to make it trickier now. Ready? North! Northeast! East! Southeast! South! Southwest! West! Northwest! And we're back to north again.*

Once the class is clear about directions, you might decide to show with your bodies: the wind blowing in the prevailing direction; winds changing and blowing from the south; rivers flowing in a direction (south from the continental divide, north from the continental divide); and storms whirling in from the west. Different children can demonstrate the winds and the rivers and each group of winds or rivers can show how it interacts with the earth:

> *Remember to use your levels—high, medium, low—and don't forget that the winds and rivers don't blow and flow in straight lines all the time. Let's see some curves, and even zigzags! I'll try to fit my drumming to your movement. Storms, are you ready?*

*Children use movement in a
geography/science lesson about rivers.*

The storms cross the room, twirling and swirling, faster and faster.

Movement can represent the landforms across the continent, the rivers and lakes, even the busy cities. The whole map of the United States can be represented with bodies that stretch tall for mountains and slither along for rivers. All the while, the children must keep referencing the map to locate the right positions for their parts of nature.

Using movement to study historical periods

You can also use movement to evoke historical periods and cultures. The circle dances of early New England or the square dances of the early West capture beautifully the lively but less intimate ways that men and women related socially in the distant past. A memorable comparison of gender expectations and norms between modern and historical Americans will become very tangible in the juxtaposition of hip hop or salsa with the Virginia reel! I still remember vividly the measured (what felt to us like stilted) movements we made in our eighth grade study of colonial America, when Georgie Williams and I led the minuet line.

Music

We can also bring a culture alive through its music. When Ghanaian musician Sowah Mensah worked as an artist-in-residence at Prairie Creek Elementary School, he taught the whole school a call-and-response song sung by people in Ghana while they work:

Call: Nah aley vee no coolo me
           Go bah bah
           Nah aley vee!

Response: Yay yay me do bah bah
           Nah aley vee!
           [Repeat above.]

Call: Nah aley vee no coolo
           Nah aley vee no coolo

Response: Yay, yay, me do bah bah
           Nah aley vee!

Sowah told us that music goes on all the time in Ghana, during work and play, and people join in whenever they feel like it. A little later that day, I overheard a boy in the library at the computer singing softly to himself, "Yay, yay, me do bah bah / Nah aley vee." There he was, just like his counterparts in Ghana, singing as he worked, and singing rhythms as old as ancient history. The rhythm of his life at school and the rhythm of the song from across the ocean had become one. A month later, the boy's whole class was singing the work song whenever they cleaned up to transition from one activity to another, in call-and-response style, with one child acting as the caller.

Because music has this way of evoking another time or culture so that you begin to know it on a feeling as well as on a rational level, it can be used to spark many topics in the social studies curriculum (for example, songs of the American Revolution, songs of the old West, songs of the American Civil War, temperance songs, and union songs).

When all the facts are reported and tested, all the concepts discussed, it will likely be the songs that will stick the longest and trigger best a memory of the *sense* of the way we used to be. Try playing *America the Beautiful* or having the students hum it softly as you read the *Preamble to the Constitution* or the *Gettysburg Address*. The emotion of music mingled with some of the finest words of our history are more powerful than either alone.

A Sample Arts-Integrated Social Studies Lesson

How do we integrate these juicy art pieces into the social studies curriculum? Here's a plan based on Margaret Burke's lesson about the social effects of a local body of water, Lake Harriet:

LESSON TOPIC:

THE LAKE HARRIET NEIGHBORHOOD (Third, fourth, fifth grades)

Goals | To understand and appreciate the ways in which a body of water can affect the life around it; to increase knowledge about the history of the neighborhood; to develop skills in careful observation and accurate recording.

Spark | Read a poem about people relating to water; tell a story about the effect of water on people who live near it; or show paintings, drawings, and/or photos of Lake Harriet and its neighborhood.

*Poetry
Storytelling
Visual arts*

Group Inquiry | Conversation about the lake and the neighborhood; chart what we know and what we are curious about. Introduction to the use of cameras. Field trip to Lake Harriet to take pictures of the lake, the parkland and streets around it, and people using it. Look at photos, reflect individually and as a group on what they show us.

Photography

Choices | Choose one way to show what you've learned:
- Write a poem, article, or story.
- Make a photo/drawing collage.
- Paint a picture from a photo.
- Make a book about Lake Harriet, using photographs or drawings to illustrate.
- Make a poster and pamphlet inviting the public to enjoy Lake Harriet.

*Book arts
Poetry
Visual arts*

Planning | Written plan; teacher signs off.

Work | Work in partners or groups no larger than four students.

Reflection and Sharing | Teach about Lake Harriet using your product. Audience asks questions, compliments the students presenting, makes suggestions if presenting students ask for them. Quiz with questions based on presentations.

*Poetry
Visual arts*

Integrating the arts into social studies gives students a range of ways to learn and to demonstrate what they've learned. For some students, drawing a Mayan temple may be much more instructive than writing about one. If the drawing is accurate and labeled carefully, it can provide a long-lasting visual memory. Singing and dancing in the style of another culture helps internalize their ways into our ways.

If we really mean to make the journey into other times and places one that prepares children to think deeply and with empathy about the others of the world, then we would be wise to use the arts to make the journey meaningful and moving.

WORKS CITED

Beal, Nancy. 2001. *The Art of Teaching Art to Children in School and at Home.* New York: Farrar, Straus, and Giroux.

Christensen, Linda. 2000. *Reading, Writing, and Rising Up: Teaching About Social Justice and the Power of the Written Word.* Milwaukee, WI: Rethinking Schools Ltd.

Keenan, Deborah, and Roseann Lloyd, eds. 1990. *Looking for Home: Women Writing About Exile.* Minneapolis: Milkweed Editions.

Randall, Karen. 1988. *The Middle Ages: An Integrated Curriculum.* Northfield, MN: Unpublished curriculum.

Using the Arts to Teach Science

Scientists and children, especially the youngest children, have something in common: they are very curious. They want to know how the physical world works and why. Our task as teachers is to keep this youthful curiosity alive—to turn "I don't know" into the starting point for investigations that are lively and rigorous. The heart of the study of science lies in the quest to know. In the classroom, the arts can help keep this quest alive and lively.

In this chapter you'll find ways to use the arts to help children:

- Make a personal response to the facts they learn about science

- Understand systems and processes

- Accurately record observations

- Learn science vocabulary

- Explore the big questions—why things happen

Movement

Movement can dramatize a science topic powerfully. Lisa Boland Blake, a teacher at Valley Crossing Community School, used movement to teach lessons that were part science, part geography. For example, she and the students used movement to understand the geography of rivers.

After the first, second, and third grade students listened to water music, they brainstormed a list of words that related to water: "rush," "drip," "flow," "bubble," "wave," "seep," "trickle," "float,"

*A student drawing of the course
of the Yellow River in China.*

"pour." They were also introduced to vocabulary words such as "headwaters," "mouth" or "source," "delta," "floodwaters," and "tributary." Then everyone drew a picture of a river, labeling its parts and showing its direction.

Now it was time to show with their bodies what they had learned. In the gym, the children had five counts to find their own spaces within the boundaries Lisa designated. They did a few warm-ups to remind themselves of how to show shapes, levels, and directions. Lisa called out some words, and the children represented them with movement: "waving," "rushing," "trickling," "whirling."

Next, in pairs and using an atlas, students drew the route of a river in China on a blank map of China and walked out the route of their river, starting from the direction where the mouth of the river is located.

*Children use their bodies to show water movement (left) and to
walk along the course of a river, following maps they drew earlier (right).*

It was time to put everything together into a dance. "Make a shape with your bodies at the source of the river," Lisa told them. "Now move along the route showing three water words and then end with another shape." After a three minute practice, partners performed for the whole group, who guessed what the water was doing along its journey and applauded the dancers.

This was a complex lesson with many elements, but children would benefit from just using movement to demonstrate the vocabulary words. The wonderful thing about movement is that even a little of it enlivens the children and deepens their learning. And simple movement demonstrations done by one or two children at a time do not require extra space and are easy to manage: *Karla and Ramon, please demonstrate for us the rotation of the moon around the earth. Now LaVon is the sun, and the earth revolves around him. Keep rotating around the earth, Ramon. In the solar system you are both moving all the time, aren't you?*

Some other science topics that lend themselves nicely to representation through movement are:

Animals moving in groups

A herd of buffalo, a pod of whales, a gaggle of geese, a swarm of bees. Five or so children at a time can demonstrate the movement of the animal after the class has discussed the nature of that movement—its speed, how far apart the animals are as they move, the dynamic of the movement (thundering, sliding, bobbing along)—or if you have access to a large space, the whole class can try one animal after another.

Body systems

Dancers move from the heart out to the extremities and back to the heart, while the teacher and students beat out the heart rhythm with drums or their feet.

Solids, liquids, and gases

A group shows the movement of molecules in all three states of matter, from the slow exchanges of a solid, to the speedier movement of liquids, to the rapid traffic of gaseous molecules.

Electrons, protons, and neutrons in an atom

The structure of an atom can be represented by varying numbers of electrons, protons, and neutrons—from the simple configuration of a hydrogen atom to the great complexity of organic matter. The protons and neutrons can jiggle a little in the center while the electrons circle around them.

Growth of a plant from a seed

"Seeds" can be distributed around the room, represented by bodies hunched over on their knees, taking up as little space as possible. Then someone comes to shine on them, and someone else sprinkles water on them, and pretty soon the seeds are germinating as represented by their extending bodies reaching towards the sky, their arms going out to show leaves, and their heads tall and proud to represent their flowers. Representation through movement can continue as the flower bears fruit, the fruit falls from the plant, and out of the fruit comes a small seed to start the process all over again.

Fulcrum and balance

Students can make a strong visual demonstration of the idea of a fulcrum if one stands with outstretched arms while others demonstrate balance (one child on each side) or imbalance (several on one side, one on the other). The fulcrum indicates the shifts in balance by tipping outstretched arms one way or another as different numbers and sizes of children load one end or the other. Or one child alone can demonstrate what happens when the center of balance shifts too far to one side or another: *stand on one foot and lean till the unevenly distributed weight pulls you over.*

Based on space or management concerns, you might decide to create these lively demonstrations with only one small group or individual, with the rest of the class watching, or have the whole class try balancing in different ways so that each child can feel the moment when the center of balance shifts and the child begins to tip over.

If you decide to try movement explorations with all of the class at once, and some lose self-control, you can have those children sit out and watch. If most start losing control, stop the exercise and say: *It looks as if not all of us have the self-control yet to manage this and follow our rules. We'll try something less demanding and hope that sometime soon we'll be able to do these kinds of movement explorations.* But keep giving the students chances to move—they will push themselves to grow in self-control just to get the chance to move.

Theater

There are many theater activities that lend themselves very well to science study. For example, some teachers use theater to help children understand and remember the body systems, as in this demonstration of digestion:

Food, in the form of children labeled with pictures of carrots and meat and milk, travels through the alimentary canal. The canal is portrayed by the rest of the group standing in two parallel lines that curve in appropriate places to suggest the mouth, pharynx, esophagus, stomach, large and small intestines, and rectum, as well as the liver and gall bladder. The moment everyone anticipates with glee is when the food emerges at the far end of the canal, transformed into you-know-what!

The same kind of vivid drama/movement works for other systems as well—the respiratory or circulatory system, photosynthesis, a representation of the solar system. Students can use their bodies to make stationary and mobile representations of all the parts that make the whole. What becomes visibly and kinesthetically clear is that each part depends upon the other for the whole system to work. With some poetic license, the literal representation can become a lyrical one: some recorded music or a student percussion ensemble, the "sun" equipped with a flashlight to shine on the "planets" (who might be dressed in dark colors), and you have the dance of the universe.

Erin Klug and her fifth grade students at Willard Elementary in Minneapolis produced a musical about magnetism one spring, with script and songs written by the children. After the class had read, discussed, experimented, and made illustrated journals about magnets and their properties, they decided to show what they had learned. They created a story about attraction and repulsion in human relationships, wrote songs, choreographed a dance, and made the sets out of recycled corrugated cardboard. They measured, drew, and cut the props and scenery. They wrote not only the script

Creating "A Tale of Two Magnets": posters, song-writing, script, scenery, invitations, displays, and finally—performance!

and the program, but descriptions of each step of their process, with illustrations and photographs, which they mounted on large pieces of poster board so that on the night of the performance their families could learn more about magnetism and about the children's learning process.

I asked Erin why she didn't simply do the display—it was elaborate and comprehensive enough to serve as an excellent culminating project in and of itself, and the making of it provided a vehicle for plenty of learning. Her response was that the musical was what sparked all the work. These fifth graders loved to sing and move and talk! Erin had decided back in September that she would have to find ways of making their energy work *for* the class instead of becoming a year full of behavior issues. The idea of doing something that included all the things they loved to do and performing in front of an audience provided just the inspiration the students needed to keep working hard all through the spring.

Simulations

Theater offers other simpler formats, such as simulated interviews, to engage students in the curriculum. You can do interviews not only with people, but with *parts* of people and with inanimate objects. Why not interview the stomach to see what it knows first hand about digestion? What does planet Neptune think about, all alone and so far away from the sun? Ask a plant what job it likes better, the photosynthesis of the daytime or the respiratory night shift? After research into the various parts of a system, the personification of the parts will both solidify learning and provide entertainment.

Using more elaborate simulations, you can help students understand some of the larger ethical issues that are part of the study of science. One day at Prairie Creek Elementary School, I walked in on a simulated town meeting in Pearl Devenow's mixed grade level classroom. The meeting focused on the issues involved in cutting down the trees of a nearby forest, Nerstrand Woods. The students had been immersed in a study of ecosystems. Now they had a chance to apply their learning to a situation where the study of ecology intersects with public policy and economics.

There were opinions from the owner of the lumber company, a bird watcher, a naturalist, a worker in the lumber company, and even from a deer, a rabbit, and a bird. With very little coaching, the children presented the case for or against, drawing on the knowledge they had about the delicate balance of ecosystems. They were completely into the role-playing and gripped enough by the question that at recess, after about forty-five minutes of hearings, they went outside and played together maintaining their roles!

What interested me most about this exercise was the passion with which the children participated. The group ranged in age from six to nine, and every one of them was fully engaged in the question of whether or not it would be advisable and just to cut down an area of old forest in an age where there are few left. Facts, ideas, and feelings—just the recipe for remembering—and theater was the key leavening agent.

Storytelling

I met a Montessori teacher once who used the technique of the "big story" to introduce science (and other) units of study. I like the tradition and imagine telling a big story to begin a study of the solar system. *How did the universe begin?* The big story might involve mythology and early theories as well as current ideas on the subject. It could be dramatic and memorable, and set the stage for learning at a feeling level as well as an intellectual one:

There was darkness and nothing else. No planet Earth twirled through the sky. No moon kept her company. There was just blackness, they say, until the moment came when a huge mass moving through the void exploded. Some say it collided with another huge mass. Others say it was shattered by a Creator who spun pieces of it into the universe as material for something very special.

And something very special did come of it—nine huge balls of matter that gathered in a beautiful pattern of nine concentric circles around the sun, some with other spheres circling them, others with rings around them, some just alone, spinning and circling. For those of us who came to inhabit the sphere later called planet Earth, it was a grand moment—the birthday of our world!

If you choose to tell a big story to introduce a unit of study, you might decide to dramatize the telling, adding some props, even sound effects or music. The idea is to launch the study in a powerful way, to create images in the minds of students that will provide a rich imaginative context for all that they will learn on that topic.

Students can also tell stories about topics they are studying. For example, the study of butterflies or birds or iguanas can culminate in student stories about a butterfly or bird that loses its way during migration or an iguana that wished its body was smooth and simple like its relative, the snake.

But in order for storytelling to demonstrate science learning, directions for the assignment must stress the importance of accuracy: *Be true to the facts you have gathered about your animal as you tell about its adventures!*

Visual Arts

Observational drawing is a much-used tool of any scientist. If children are going to think as scientists think, and begin to develop the work habits of the scientific method, they need to learn the art of accurate rendering. A focus on the techniques of observational drawing will empower them to do that. It will actually help them to see what they look at.

When we introduce children to observational drawing, they concentrate very hard—even the youngest ones. They are pleased when what they have drawn looks like what is before them, and except for the five- and six-year-olds, they take great care in coloring their pencil or pen drawings to maintain that accuracy. But if the goal is accuracy, it's important to use an easily-controlled material like colored pencils. It's not that paint, crayon, and charcoal are not good materials to use; it's a matter of deciding what your objectives are in any particular lesson, and making a clear distinction: Are we drawing for accuracy? Are we drawing for expression? Are we going for both?

In order to sharpen the observational strengths of a group of fifth and sixth graders, I took them outside to look at a tree that grew just beside the school. Here are the instructions I gave:

Look at this tree carefully. Notice its size, structure, and the details of its leaf shape and arrangement on the branches. We're going inside in a few minutes to draw the tree, so use this time to print its image into your memory so you'll have what you need to draw it accurately.

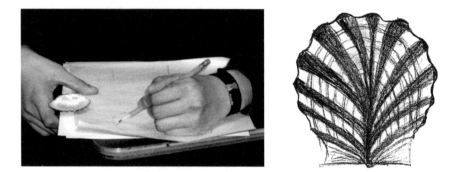

A seventh-grader accurately draws a shell,
something simple in shape and rich in texture.

After a few minutes we went inside to draw. There were lots of mumbled comments and sighs. The students were not happy with their drawings. So we went outside again and took another look before returning to the drawings. This time students were much more focused in their looking, trying to fill in the gaps they had discovered in their visual memories of the trees. Finally, we went out with clip boards and finished the drawings while looking at the tree. The students were pleased with their final drawings, and I knew that the two attempts to draw by visual memory had sharpened their capacity to really see what was before them and to record its details accurately.

Other applications of drawing to science are easy to think of: geologic studies of the earth's crust; the parts of a microscope; dissection drawings; images of the solar system; rock specimens; diagrams of experiments with levers, pulleys, and fulcrums. In each case the emerging scientists need to observe sharply and record accurately, often with labels.

To do so successfully, they need drawing as well as spelling and writing lessons, with at least enough practice in accurate rendering to get them started in the right direction. Continued practice, combined with assessment (self, peer, and teacher) does the rest.

Children are proud of these kinds of projects—they enjoy having something to show for their work in learning, something attractive as well as instructive. And of course for those students whose natural bent is visual, the scientific drawings become a way that their knowledge can shine through and inspire others.

Record and respond

Of course accuracy is only one thing we are trying to cultivate in young scientists. We also want them to develop a sense of the context within which a plant or animal lives, its ecosystem. And we want them to make some kind of personal connection to the natural world, a connection that will inspire future investigations, scientific and otherwise, a connection that will make the work we are doing meaningful and therefore deeper and more memorable.

To move beyond observational drawing, I often ask children to add line or color to their representational drawings, using a medium other than the pencil or pen with which they have recorded:

> *Show us this plant or animal in the world. Show how it feels or how you feel about it. If you were to add color to give your woodland creature a place to live, what color would you choose?*

You can then give the children oil pastels, crayons, colored pencils, or watercolors, and after a guided exploration into this material so that they will know how to use it well, let them create a world in which their accurately-drawn plant or creature can live.

They love this part, of course. Their pleasure in the results derives from that combination of accurate rendering plus imaginative elaboration which I call "record and respond." The wholeness of it leaves them empowered to see carefully, represent exactly, and expand what they know into what they feel and sense.

My favorite book on education, *In the Early World: Discovering Art Through Crafts* by New Zealand author Elwyn Richardson, illustrates how drawing can help children make a personal connection to science. Richardson describes how he purchased a low-powered microscope that gave a wide field of about X10 magnification:

> This microscope added great possibilities to nature study and brought within our range of experience almost anything that the children observed. We found, too, that the beauties of small seeds and insects were most startling. For instance, the seeds of vervain were found to be extremely beautiful.
>
> Drawing of designs from these observations became just as much a part of nature work as the writing of poetry did at a later time.... (Richardson 1964, 57–58)

Richardson's book is full of the linocuts his students made from the nature that they observed. Eventually, the drawings became printed fabric which became aprons and pinafores, curtains, and cushions. The stuff of school became the stuff of their lives.

Using other visual art forms

Visual images can help children gain clear understanding and remember just about any aspect of science. Meri Gauthier's third and fourth grade science classes at Barton Open School in Minneapolis studied the skeletal structure by creating skeletal models out of tagboard, then putting the models in humanoid positions. "Choose a position you can imitate with your own body, so you know it's possible," Meri reminded them.

*The student who did this drawing used ink for an accurate record
of the shapes and crayon for colorful self-expression.*

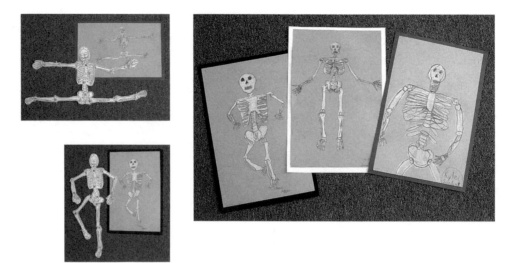

Students made paper skeletons and drew the skeletons in various positions as part of a study of bones and joints (see the Sample Lesson at the end of the chapter).

Once the students decided on a position for the figure, they used white oil pastels on black construction paper to catch the gesture of the figure. The result was drawings that for the most part were both accurate and engaging. At the end of the chapter, you'll find Meri's lesson written up in the arts-integrated lesson plan format.

Architectural constructions

Meri also likes to challenge the students to make architectural constructions. To do so, they discover principles of physics and mathematics, like any good architect who must have a working knowledge of structural engineering in order to design a building. On the following page are illustrations of two building projects done by Meri's students, one of which culminated in drawings of the buildings and the other in sculptural representations.

The students' buildings can be fanciful ones, just as long as in the designing and making of them, students are learning and following structural design principles. In the drawings, students were given the assignment of creating a building design using a basic shape which they would then be allowed to flip, slide, or rotate into different positions. These translations would become the structural pieces of the buildings.

In the sculptural project, students looked at geodesic domes and then used nails and clay to make a structure that would depart from the omnipresent box design of most buildings. Students used triangles, rectangles, and other polygons to design their buildings out or up, in cantilevered and spiraled constructions. In the process, they learned first-hand about the laws of physics. "The clay will let you know when you've gone too far," Meri told them. Afterwards they discussed principles of thrust and balance deduced from their explorations. The handsome sculptures themselves were a tribute to the marriage of science and art.

*Drawn and sculptural representations of building designs from
students in Meri Gauthier's third/fourth grade science classes.*

Mixed media

My daughter Elizabeth Crawford, an artist who loves science, has had older students study
the growth of the human embryo from seed to birth. They read about and discussed the steps:
egg + sperm, dividing cells, blastocyst, two weeks, five weeks, ten weeks, and the physical
transformations—from a zygote to an embryo to a fetus to a fully-equipped human being. It was
all clearly presented and well understood, thanks to the large accumulation of information (including
in utero photographs) that exists on the subject.

The students had the facts. All that were missing were the miracle and the mystery. We know
it happens, but why? How can it be that such a thing is possible, that sperm seek eggs and that
their union sets off an amazing multiplication and differentiation of cells? What is the experience
of womb life?

Elizabeth helped her students investigate such questions by extending their investigation into
the world of the imagination. They made a series of to-scale clay fetuses to show the stages of
embryo growth. Elizabeth then invited them to create an imaginary environment for the clay models. Students set the models in gauze, net, glass, and paper worlds of their own making, and then
photographed them, often using photographer's tricks such as point of view and intentional dis-
tortion through focus and depth-of-field, to capture something of what it might feel like inside the
womb. The results were mysterious and moving—imagination and science connecting to evoke the
miracle of new life.

Poetry

Textbooks, labs, and field trips give children lots of information about the biological world and scientific processes, but when children write a poem about what they've learned, they move beyond facts to contemplate what the new knowledge means to them. Poetry then becomes their response to what they have recorded.

One summer in a program for third to fifth grade students, visiting educator Chip Wood, the classroom teachers, and I combined photography and poetry with a study of the ecology of the prairie. We took a field trip to a preserved piece of original Minnesota prairie land. With students equipped with point-and-shoot cameras (one per pair) and paper sun hats, we walked the length of this small piece of prairie and marveled at the life that teemed in the swaying grasses under a cloudless sky. When the children returned, they wrote poems about their experiences and made cyanotype contact prints using the negatives processed from their film. They also made drawings of the prairie plants that grow in the model prairie on the school grounds and made photograms with plant material pressed against specially-treated paper and exposed to sunlight.

The results were delicately beautiful. We put together an exhibition that not only informed viewers about the prairie, but evoked it for them. The children gave us not just what they saw, but what they imagined and felt:

> The Prairie is so silent like a corpse.
> Wind blows the grass as easily as a person whistles.
> Buffalo sleeping, dreaming about food.
> —*Sixth grader*

> I am just a dot against the sky, not immortal.
> Not as this thing I feel near me.
> Maybe it's the wind, but I don't think so.
> —*Fifth grader*

(In Chapter 7, you'll find writing formats you can use to inspire imaginative responses to science investigations.)

It is this elaborating on information that makes the content areas truly rich—science (like social studies, math, reading, and writing) learned through observation, open-ended thinking, and renderings that evoke the beauty as well as the facts of the world.

A Sample Arts-Integrated Science Lesson

Here is Meri Gauthier's lesson about the skeleton, described in our lesson planner:

LESSON TOPIC: HUMAN SKELETON

(Third, fourth, fifth grades)

Goals
To understand and appreciate the flexibility and adaptability of the human skeletal structure; to know the number and nature of joints in the body; to learn the names of the bones in the body.

Spark
One student will demonstrate different body positions, and another will manipulate a jointed skeletal figure to imitate the demonstrator's positions. Then the demonstrating student will try to imitate a few positions that the skeleton is put into.

Movement

Group Inquiry
Questions: What did you notice about what Peter could do with the skeleton figure? What about Andrea—could she do all of those things with her body? What seem to be some of the limits of our body's skeletal movements?

Demonstration of 3-step process: 1) get your body into a position; 2) put the skeleton into that same position (or ask your partner to do it while you hold the position; 3) draw the skeleton's position showing all the joints.

Movement Drawing

Choices
• Partners or alone.
• Position of the skeleton.
• Color combinations [Meri chose to have everyone do white on black, but you could offer more choice in color of oil pastels and/or construction paper.]

Movement Drawing

Planning
Students will use planning paper to sketch their skeletal figure before drawing it on the construction paper, so they can get the proportions correct. Teacher will sign off on the sketches, looking for proportion and accuracy about what a joint can actually do.

Drawing

Work
• Can use partners for positioning skeletal figure, but all students will do a drawing on their own.
• Work on tables only (floor doesn't allow for good drawing position).
• Two science periods, maybe three.

Reflection and Sharing
Exhibition of finished work. Sharing: Student who did a drawing stands by figure with his/her body in position of the figure. Questions: Is student accurately representing the figure s/he has drawn? What corrections if any need to be made? Has the student demonstrated that this is indeed a position the human body can assume? Student names the bones and joints in the skeleton image.

Movement Drawing

Work Cited

Richardson, Elwyn S. 1964. *In the Early World: Discovering Art Through Crafts.* New York: Pantheon Books.

Using the Arts
to Teach Math

Success with math depends on remembering lots of information. The emerging mathematician has to memorize counting, prime numbers, algorithms for solving problems, formulas for finding the area of geometric figures, algebraic formulas. The higher in math you go, the more there is to remember. Frank Smith, author of *The Book of Learning and Forgetting,* has a strategy for putting new knowledge into long-term memory. "You put something into long-term memory," he says, "by finding a structure for it that already exists in your head; by making sense of it, in other words." (Smith 1998, 33) The arts can give children a familiar structure that helps them learn and remember what numbers are and what they can do.

In this chapter you'll find strategies for using movement, music, storytelling, and drawing to help students learn about and practice working with varied aspects of math, such as:

- Basic counting and computation

- Fractions

- Ratio

- Polygons

- Graphing

Perhaps even more important, many of the arts strategies presented in this chapter make math more appealing and less anxiety-producing for children.

Movement

Movement, which is concrete, can help children understand abstract mathematical concepts. For example, movement can help young students understand crucial math vocabulary:

Larger

Students make their bodies expand by stretching up and out, or groups cluster together to make bigger groups.

Smaller

Students pull their bodies in, "shrink" them by taking up less space, or groups break into groups of fewer people.

Greater than/lesser than

Two groups—one larger, one smaller—face each other across a line. The larger group makes expansive movements; the smaller pulls together and shrinks in.

Least, more, and most

To demonstrate "least," one person out of a group stands. For "more," others join the first person. For "most," all but a few of the group stand. Everyone chants the correct term as each step happens. Then the group turns "most" back into "least" by having the last two groups to stand sit down again (leaving the one child standing), then "least" back to "more" by a few others standing, and so on, practicing the terms mentally, verbally, and physically until everyone has them.

Here are some other ideas for using movement to help you and the children enjoy math lessons and anchor your math abstractions.

Using movement to practice counting

Gathered in a circle, children move around the ring using their feet to stamp out the numbers: one, two, three, four, five, six, seven, eight, nine, ten. They continue marching as they count to fifty, letting the rhythm of their bodies reinforce the numbers their mouths are saying. They get to feel the difference between fifty and twenty—it's several more times around the circle, and 100 feels like a much bigger number than little old ten.

To prepare for computation with numbers, the children can count and accent numbers at certain intervals ("skip counting"):

- Counting by twos: *One,* two, *three,* four, *five,* six, *seven,* eight.

- Counting by threes: *One,* two, three; *four,* five, six; *seven,* eight, nine.

Liz Hagedorn, a fourth grade teacher in Minneapolis, integrates movement into math four days a week. Concerned that her students didn't get enough experience with large numbers, she challenged them to begin with 100 and literally skip as they counted by fives: 100 [skip skip skip skip] 105 [skip skip skip skip] 110 and so on.

Using movement to increase engagement with math

Movement activities might also help the math-anxious students in a class feel more comfortable. Although students still need to do the work of computation and problem solving, reluctant students are motivated to do this work because they know they'll get to show their answers through movement. Students stay stimulated and engaged, and the exercise even contributes oxygen to their computation center—the frontal lobes.

Fact triangles

A potentially dry lesson in addition and subtraction becomes fun and interesting when students use fact triangles to physically demonstrate number sentences.

Three children, each with a different one-digit number pinned on him or her, form a triangle. Let's say the numbers are five, two, and seven, which can form the following number sentences:

$$5 + 2 = 7$$
$$2 + 5 = 7$$
$$7 - 5 = 2$$
$$7 - 2 = 5$$

The group of three decides on a movement to make such as hopping, leaping, or bowing. Then as the whole class (or the individual wearing the number or the small group) says the number sentence (slowly), the child who represents each number makes the agreed-on movement: "Five [number five makes a hop] plus two [number two hops] equals seven [number seven hops]." The audience sees and hears (and possibly speaks) the computation; the group performing actually feels it.

Balance points

You can also have fun with movement through an activity that uses balance points to show whole number answers to problems such as "4 + 4 - 5 = ?". Students first solve the problem and then show their answers to others by getting into weird positions and holding them. Allison Rubin Forester demonstrated this technique to a group of teachers in an Origins arts-integration workshop and the teachers loved it.

Balance points are the points at which the body touches the floor. For example, standing on two feet equals two balance points; standing on one foot equals one balance point; standing on two feet and bending over to touch the floor with one hand equals three balance points, etc. The teacher writes a problem on the board, individuals or pairs solve the problem, and then get into a body position where the number of balance points equals the answer to the problem. In the problem stated earlier, students would need to show three balance points.

It's most fun to do balance points in pairs who stay physically connected to each other (leaning on each other, holding hands, etc.). To show the answer to the problem stated earlier, "4 + 4 - 5 = 3," two students could start out by facing each other and holding hands. Then one student could lift a foot off the floor, leaving three balance points. If the pair is demonstrating the answer for the whole class, a volunteer from the class can say the number of balance points she observes.

Before giving all the students in the class a chance to do the exercise, it's a good idea to ask for two students to demonstrate the activity while you talk them through it. Then have a brief discussion about how the demonstrators did the task successfully: *What did you notice about the way they helped each other?* One student might notice that the two held hands and leaned towards each other. *You can help each other out any way that is safe and respectful. I'll be checking and helping as you work.*

When everyone in the class has had a chance to solve a given problem and figure out their balance points, each individual or pair can demonstrate their answer by freezing in their balance points position. The class can indicate whether they agree or disagree with the answer and why.

Once you've introduced the idea of showing a number with your body, and practiced it a little bit, you can use balance points anytime you want to add fun and a little exercise to a math lesson.

Using movement to learn graphing

Another math lesson that lends itself easily to movement is graphing. First, students gather data about the class—how many birthdays in each quarter of the year; how many children with zero, one, two, three, four, or more siblings, pets, cousins; numbers of people who prefer chocolate, vanilla, strawberry, or other flavors of ice cream, etc. After the data is gathered, students line up to make live graphs of the results for each category: ten children line up at the "chocolate" point, four at the "vanilla" point, five at "strawberry," etc. Afterwards, in responding to questions such as which line represents the most popular ice cream flavor, the appropriate line in the graph makes a movement in place—something like leaning from side to side or marching in place.

This bar graph becomes more vivid
when students line up to make a live graph.

Using movement to understand fractions

This is an exercise you would do in a large space if everyone is going to try it, or you could do a demonstration with sixteen (or eight) children in front of the class—a lot quicker and, of course, easier to control.

To do this with sixteen children, the group demonstrating stands in four parallel lines of four people each. Each line decides on one in-place movement that the children in that line will make in succession. The teacher draws the "dance" on a chart or the board by writing down (in a four-by-four array) the movements that each line decided on:

point	hop	sway	spin
point	hop	sway	spin
point	hop	sway	spin
point	hop	sway	spin

First the group performs all sixteen steps, one line at a time, person by person in sequence: point, point, point, point; hop, hop, hop, hop, sway, etc. Then the first line sits down, and the remaining three lines dance twelve steps: hop, hop, hop, hop, sway, sway, sway, sway, etc. On the chart, the teacher circles the "point" group and asks how many lines of children sat down. The children will answer that one of the lines sat down, or 1/4 of the lines. The teacher can then ask how many lines are left, with the answer being 3/4 of the lines.

Next the second line sits, so now only the third and fourth lines are left. They perform their steps:

How many lines are now sitting down?

Two out of the four or 2/4.

You could also talk about fractions of sixteen:

Let's talk about the steps in the dance now. There were sixteen movements to begin with. How much of the dance did we just perform?

Eight steps out of the sixteen, or 8/16.

And so on, playing with the numbers, doing and watching the movement, getting an increasingly better sense with our bodies of what fractions are really all about.

Using movement to understand ratio

Ratio is another abstract concept that students can illustrate using movement. Consider the following typical word problem:

William and Turrel are both riding their bikes to their cousins' houses. William's cousin Deloris lives only two miles from his house, but the way is mostly uphill, so he averages only five miles per hour. Turrel's cousin Damone lives four miles from his house, but the way is mostly flat, so he averages twelve miles per hour. William and Turrel each left home at nine a.m. Who will get to his cousin's house first?

In order to answer this problem correctly, children need to understand the mathematical concept of ratio, in this case the relationship between distance and time as represented by the term "miles per hour." They also need to understand the concept that travel time is a function of both speed and distance. Otherwise they might jump to the erroneous conclusion that since Turrel had further to go, he would arrive later.

How do you get such concepts into your head? It helps a lot to translate them into the real world, which we can perceive with our senses. Let's set up a demonstration of the impact of speed on travel time. We'll have two students—Jamie (representing William) and Robin (representing Turrel)—travel across the room. Jamie will begin halfway across the room and hop on one foot; Robin will begin all the way across the room and will skip:

Who got to the other side first?

Robin.

How come?

'Cause she was going faster?

But she had farther to travel.

Yeah, but when you go faster, you get there sooner.

So what you are telling us is that even when two people are traveling different distances, you can't tell who will get to the destination first unless you can describe how fast each of them is going?

And from there we go into setting up a standard for this relationship called "miles per hour" (mph) that will help children solve the original word problem. Some children do not need the demonstration with movement to understand the concept, but it will still make the mathematical relationships more vivid to them. Others can't understand mph without it. At the very least, the movement demonstration will have drawn their attention to the physical reality that is intrinsic to the abstract numbers in the problem.

Using movement to understand polygons

Movement is particularly useful for studying geometry. For example, children can discover polygons with their own bodies and then, once they've explored and formed the shapes, they can name them. To make certain that everyone knows what different kinds of polygons look like, begin by displaying large (9x12) drawings of the shapes you will ask students to create with their bodies. Then tell students that they will be using their bodies to make these shapes, beginning with the square.

First, identify the key elements of the shape: numbers of sides, numbers and locations of vertices. Then invite four volunteers to form a square. They might stand, one on each side facing inwards, and raise their arms out to the side, or they might lie down, with one student's head touching another student's feet at each vertex. As soon as the four are in place, another student can come up and count the sides of their shape, identify the vertices, and name the shape.

Next, have everybody practice the square in groups of four. Once they have successfully made a square, you can move on to other shapes. Begin by assigning shapes to each group; but as a final experience, students can make their own shapes. Just be sure they understand that the shapes need to have a clear number of straight sides and visible vertices. And as groups spread out around the room, remind them about moving safely within their own bubble of space.

At the end of the work period, each group can come to the front of the room and make their assigned or designed shape while you (or a student) draws the shape on the board. The class then gets to count the sides and vertices and name the shape while you label the shape on the board.

In many of these movement exercises, children will work independently in small groups and then demonstrate the results of their work in front of the large group. Some students might feel reluctant to do this but it's a good idea to encourage them to try. Allison Rubin Forester, an eighth grade math teacher at Barton Open School in Minneapolis, often uses movement to teach complex mathematical concepts. She says:

> Even though students may initially be self-conscious, after a while it is often students who have up to that time been unsuccessful, especially with the more abstract aspects of learning, who may understand the [movement] concepts presented and be willing, even excited to perform. These students may find, as many have, that they are beginning to really understand complex ideas and they are having fun at the same time. (Forester 2000)

Music

Jane Gravender, a kindergarten teacher at Webster Open School in Minneapolis, sings with her five- and six-year-old students a lot. One of their favorite ways to learn to say and write numbers is a number song sung to the tune of *Skip to My Lou:*

> Number 1: Come right down and let it go
> Come right down and let it go
> Come right down and let it go
> To make the number 1!
>
> Number 2: Curve around and slide to the right
> Curve around and slide to the right
> Curve around and slide to the right
> To make the number 2!

As the children sit in the circle and sing, their fingers trace the shape of the numeral on a piece of blank paper in front of them. They also might actually write the number as they sing at their desks, but Jane finds that when children sing and learn with each other in a circle they are better able to exercise their self-control *and* have fun. They can watch each other, pick up the words (many are English language learners), and copy the correct gestures from the children next to them (just be sure they don't copy the gestures of the children opposite them). Mostly what the children gain from the number-writing is the somatic memory of the shape. We could say that their *fingers* remember the shape of the numbers.

Using rhythm to learn and remember math

Rhythm is also a powerful tool for learning and remembering math. I've seen fourth graders commit the multiplication tables to memory (finally!) by chanting them in an even rhythm as they marched around in a circle. The rhythm and numbers curl around each other and roll into the brain together.

By exploring rhythm, children can also explore the relationships of numbers to one another. In a waltz or polka, for example, one out of every three notes is emphasized, and one out of three is easy to describe by 1/3.

Simple musical supports to math come in early childhood counting songs (*One, Two, Buckle My Shoe; One, Two, Three, O'Leary O; Green Grow the Rushes, Ho*). And rhythmic chants make subtraction easier:

> Five little monkeys
> Jumping on the bed.
> One fell out and bumped his head!
> Mama called the doctor and the doctor said,
> "No more monkeys jumping on the bed!"
> Four little monkeys
> Jumping on the bed
> One fell out and bumped his head!
> Mama called the doctor and the doctor said,
> "No more monkeys jumping on the bed!"

And so on, with children subtracting themselves off a blanket on the floor.

Last week I watched a group of first graders standing in a circle doing skip counting by twos, chanting the numbers all the way up to fifty. When they were finished and getting ready for lunch, I said to two of the boys, "I know a cheer about counting by twos." They looked at me quizzically. Taking that for an invitation, I burst into my old camp cheer which I hadn't said aloud for fifty years:

> Two, four, six, eight
> Who do we appreciate?
> **The waiters! The waiters!**
> Hip, hip the waiters!

Fun plus a tune or chant equals remembering. No matter how silly or how long ago we learned them, the rhythms and tunes apparently make things stick, so why not use them? Like you, I'll help students learn any way I can, and singing their way to graduation might be the royal route to success for a lot of children.

Storytelling and Drawing

I remember a subtraction lesson I taught to a large group of seven- and eight-year-olds. I decided to invite them into math through the doorways of storytelling and drawing: "Once there was a boy named Alexander whose aunt and uncle gave him and his two brothers a dollar each when they came to visit for a day." I retold the story from Judith Viorst's book *Alexander, Who Used to Be Rich Last Sunday*, about an impulsive boy who spent all his money frivolously, chagrined that his brothers held on to theirs. The children nodded knowingly as I catalogued all the places and ways Alexander parted with his money. Five-cent fine for using a bad word. Ten cents at a garage sale. Fifteen cents for holding his friend's pet snake, and so on. (Viorst 1988)

As I told the story, I drew on a large piece of chart paper a map of the houses and street corners, garages and stores where Alexander parted from his money. I also kept a tab going for Alexander. Starting at a dollar, every time he spent something I asked a student to subtract that amount on our running tab, until at the end of the tale, Alexander and the score hit zero.

Different students came up during the course of the story to draw and subtract—DeShon, for example:

> DeShon said, "I'm not so good at drawing houses," so I coached him through the lines he needed to show perspective.
>
> All fifty children watched with silent attention.
>
> DeShon put down the marker, stepped back, and said, "Hey, that's OK."
>
> "How much did the candy he bought at that store cost him, DeShon?"
>
> "Oh yeah—twenty-five cents. Let's see, that's take away 25 from 60 ...."
>
> DeShon worked his way through "borrowing," and sat down with satisfaction.

When it was time for the children to create their own spending stories, maps, and score cards, no one needed any prodding. The buzz of fifty gainfully-employed subtracting storytellers filled the room. Even the children who were English language learners seemed to need little help getting started. The visuals had made the story clear, and they knew their task. The drawings and story, speaking to the natural childhood eagerness for things visual and narrative, had created an opening into the abstractions of math that none of the children resisted passing through.

Narrative combined with visual images is a perfect support for figuring out word problems. Patti Bauer and Brenda Krings, second grade teachers from Mead Elementary School in Wisconsin Rapids, Wisconsin, have their students make up a story using numbers and then draw it. Everyone begins: "On my way home from the park, I saw ...." They then use numbers to describe not only things they saw, but parts of those things, and then often parts of those parts. At the end, they turn their story into multiplication questions and answer those questions with diagrams and numbers. For example:

> On my way home from the park I saw four trees with ten apples on each tree. On each apple there were six dots. How many trees in all? How many apples in all? How many dots in all?

*A picture about springtime provides an enjoyable opportunity
for students to show their understanding of fractions.*

4 trees in all x 10 apples per tree = 40 apples in all.

40 apples in all x 6 dots per apple = 240 dots on apples.

Sometimes an image alone can tell the story and teach the lesson, as in the following example on fractions from teachers Patti and Brenda:

Make a spring picture by following the directions.

1. Make five clouds in the sky.

   Make 1/5 of the clouds gray.

2. Draw four trees.

   Put pink flowers on 2/4 of the trees.

3. Draw the sun in the sky.

   Make seven rays around the sun.

4. Draw eight flowers.

   Color 1/8 of the flowers yellow.

   Color 2/8 of the flowers red.

   Color 3/8 of the flowers blue.

Color 2/8 of the flowers orange.

5. Draw three children.

   Make 1/3 of the children girls.

   Make 2/3 of the children boys.

6. Make one pet in the picture.

7. Make two kites in the sky.

   Make 1/2 of the kites red.

   Make 1/2 of the kites purple.

8. Make sure the grass is green.

WELCOME SPRING!

A Sample Arts-Integrated Math Lesson

Integrating the arts into math can be as simple as giving children the chance to draw on the morning message chart, as Margie Dorshorst, principal at Mead Elementary School did:

"How did you feel about having a day off on Friday? Turn a circle into a face to show your feeling!"

Later at the morning meeting, the children counted the number that seemed happy and those that seemed sad, and decided which was greater and lesser.

For more extensive lessons, you may wish to create a detailed written plan. As an example, on the following page is the plan for the math lesson on spending money, described earlier:

Drawing on the morning message board gives children the chance to express their feelings. Later they can analyze the results.

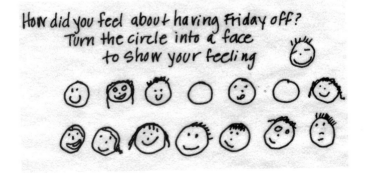

LESSON TOPIC: KEEPING TRACK OF YOUR MONEY

(Second, third grades)

Goals | To increase student skills in adding and subtracting money; to improve listening comprehension; to develop the capacity to apply an idea.

Spark | Do demonstration using *Alexander, Who Used To Be Rich Last Sunday* text, storytelling, and drawing on big chart the places Alexander spends his money. Keep a tab.

Storytelling
Drawing

Group Inquiry | Elicit some examples of times when the students had money to spend, and how they kept track of it. Why is addition and subtraction important in our lives?

Choices | Make up a story about spending money with a sequence of spending events. Choose the medium you will use for showing the events: cartoon story, map, book, model, flow chart.

Planning | Use storyboard to draw &/or write the story. Do math on separate sheet.

Drawing

Work | Work in partners. Teacher circulates to hear the stories and see that students are on track. Check that the stories are not so long and intricate that children will have trouble presenting them. Make suggestions, ask questions, and then sign off on the plans, while students begin drawing and computing. If students finish early, have them practice the presentation of their story to the class.

Storytelling
Visual arts

Reflection and Sharing | Results sheet with questions about their process. Opportunities to "teach" their story to the class; audience participates by keeping track of the spending (doing the subtraction/addition and then comparing results to the storyteller's results). Focus question: Do you think these would be wise ways to spend your money? Why?

Storytelling
Visual arts

Math is basically a description of the physical world. These various arts-integration suggestions are all designed to bring an element of that real world into the study of numbers so that budding mathematicians will be drawn to it.

WORKS CITED

Forester, Allison Rubin. 2000. *"Get 'em Moving!" Building Academic Communities through the Arts Guidelines*. Minneapolis: Origins.

Smith, Frank. 1998. *The Book of Learning and Forgetting*. New York: Teachers College Press.

Viorst, Judith. 1988. *Alexander, Who Used to Be Rich Last Sunday*. New York: Aladdin Books.

CHAPTER 14

Imaginative Understanding: Learning as a Creative Act

"The Woman Who Lives in the Sun" is a stonecut print with the face of a handsome Inuit woman in red ink floating on a piece of rice paper "as thin as the shell of a snowbird's egg." Traditional Inuit tattoo lines radiate from her mouth to her chin, and sensuous flames project from her. She is ordinary and extraordinary. The artist who drew her, Kenojuak, one of the most accomplished and well-known of the contemporary Canadian Inuit artists, creates her images out of what she sees around her, as well as what she can't see, but senses is there. What Kenojuak and the others are striving for in their work is "sananguac," a little reality. The best of their art is an imaginative rendering of what is real in their lives made large and splendid by thoughts that rush over them "like wings of birds in darkness."

"Life itself," says Kenojuak, "is not easily understood." (Feeney 1963)

Like all successful people, the traditional Inuit paid close attention to their world, understood and named what they needed, and used it creatively. That's just what we want to teach our children to do. We want our young people to get good at paying careful attention to the world, too, discerning its details and skillfully recording and using what they see and understand. But to become fully educated, with the power to think for themselves in a confusing world, make good decisions, and create something new, we need to offer them learning beyond these skills. We need to help them imagine.

Paying attention and discerning the distinctions in life can be said to consist largely, though not entirely, of what Sylvia Ashton-Warner describes as "breathing in": coming in on a topic or object of study to observe, record, analyze, and otherwise scrutinize it in order to know it very well. *Imaginative* understanding, however, comes from "breathing out": extending out from a topic or object of study to question it, alter it, or create something new. (Ashton-Warner 1963)

The processes associated with imaginative understanding are:

imagining	wondering	creating something new
connecting	messing around	inventing
playing	expressing	responding

Such is the stuff of a child experimenting with a new paper airplane design or mixing new colors or inventing silly rhymes—the stuff of an artist's work. Artists move back and forth freely between the world as it seems to others and their own personal interpretations, their thoughts and feelings. They boldly include not just what seems certain, but all the confusions and uncertainties as well. They make connections between facts and fictions, the serious and the hilarious, what everyone knows and what the artist just thought of a moment ago. When you think and work like an artist you see what only you at that moment—with your mind loose and wondering—can see, and you tell us all about it.

Throughout this book there are many suggestions for ways to integrate arts experiences into the curriculum, any one of which can facilitate learning. But doing an art activity does not necessarily mean you're thinking and working like an artist—not all art experiences open the door to imaginative understanding. For example, observational drawing helps children look closely and record accurately—to breathe in; but it doesn't necessarily invite imagination unless we add a chance to breathe out by creating an original drawing or playing with an image. Some of the time, you and the children can explore imaginatively by making interesting connections, wondering about the world together, or making stuff up.

Breathing Out:
Making Connections

When we weave subjects together and invite personal, feeling-based response we get fresh thinking and intellectual excitement. In fact, some of our best thinking comes from having the freedom to discern relationships. As new information comes into our brains, we make meaning by seeking connections to what we already know. We can hardly understand the information, much less use and remember it, unless we can connect it to other information, to feelings, to how we understand the world so far, to an association or image that flies through our minds at the moment.

In *"The Having of Wonderful Ideas" and Other Essays on Teaching and Learning*, Eleanor Duckworth writes, "David Hawkins has said of curriculum development 'You don't want to cover a subject; you want to uncover it.' That, it seems to me, is what schools should be about. They can help to uncover parts of the world that children would not otherwise know how to tackle." (Duckworth 1996, 7) A teacher's job, as Duckworth sees it, is to help children explore, question, and investigate a rich environment. We provide the materials and the questions. They snoop around, pay close attention, connect one thing to another, and respond to questions that jostle them past the obvious.

Working with integrated thematic curriculum units is one way to precipitate connections. These units may be major ones that extend for months, such as a study of the ocean, the role it plays in literature and history as well as in weather, transportation, food supply, and survival. They might also be mini-units that take a shorter journey into topics like triangles in geometry, in architecture, and in art.

You can also spark connections by means of quick games or the integration of arts activities into subject area lessons. And when more than one art medium is involved, it is hard to stop the connections from coming. For example, when we play a piece of music as background to the reading of a poem or speech, we intensify and even clarify the mood and meaning of the poem and force ourselves to view it as something akin but different. It's like those really good conversations we have when multiple points of view add layers of meaning.

So mix it up. Let the suggestions and examples in this book guide you as you invite your students to draw in history, sing in math, dance in science. My first-grade granddaughter, for example, is learning the four arithmetic processes through colorful stories about Pasha Plus, Misha Minus, Tasha Times, and Disha Divide. She learns to make her letters through stories of balmy beaches and zany zebras, accompanied by drawings adapted to the letter shapes. The arts let her connect the things she knows to each other and to what she imagines about them and in the process make new learning more accessible, meaningful, and memorable.

First graders combine storytelling with
drawing to learn and practice arithmetic.

Breathing Out:
Wondering and Questioning

We can also use the arts to introduce students to the pleasures of not-knowing. We spend a lot of our time in school coaxing children towards the right answers. But if we want children to understand through imagination as well as through logic, we need to balance single-minded certainty with open-ended questions for which not even the teacher has the "right" answer. Young people especially need to spend time in not-knowing so that they learn how to gather information from multiple sources, defer judgment until all the evidence is in, and make good choices after lengthy consideration. If we help them tolerate the gray tones in life, they may avoid falling into the rut of blindly-held, entrenched opinions.

Wonder journals

Keeping a "wonder journal" is one way to help children think in this inquiring, slightly musing, drifting-from-thought-to-thought way characteristic of creative people. New ideas and images pop into a mind let loose from correct answers. The children may not develop a new theory of the beginning of the universe, but they will begin to get some sense of how a creative mind works.

In their wonder journal, children can write questions and thoughts, pose answers when and if they think of any, draw a picture of something they're studying, maybe even doodle. And to further cultivate a climate of inquiry in the classroom, children can share entries from wonder journals at writer's workshop, morning meetings, closing the day meetings, or at the beginning, middle, or end of lessons.

Here are examples of using wonder journals to begin and end a science lesson on bees:

To introduce the lesson

We're going to study bees and how they live and work together. What are you curious about? Write your questions in your journals. Think what it might be like to be a bee! Write down your thoughts. Some of you might like to observe bees and include some drawings in your journal. Be ready to share your favorite entries with us.

To end the lesson

Now that we've learned so much about bees, what are you thinking about? Are you wondering about other insects? Other animals? What is a question you still have about bees? What is a silly or puzzled thought you've had about insects? Write these questions and thoughts in your journals.

A wonder journal encourages both teacher and children to begin with questions and also end with them.

Ending with questions

I've thought for a long time that the traditional K(Know) W(Want to know) L(Learned) sheets should really be KWLW instead: What do you already know? What do you want to know? What have you learned? Now what do you want to know? This is the spirit of inquiry that is at the heart of good learning.

This kind of inquiry is stimulated by open-ended questions such as the following:

"Chain of Lakes" questions

This describes a flow of questions in which the answer to one question becomes the source of another question. For example: How are opossum babies different from many other mammals when they are first born? Does living in a mother's pouch give more or less security than living on the ground? Rabbits move about and feed themselves very soon after their birth. Does this show that they are more or less vulnerable than baby opossums?

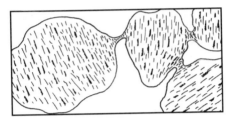

"Zoom Lens" questions

This describes questions which take us deeper and deeper into a topic. For example: Describe the Mississippi River in the Twin Cities area. What is the water like along Park? Does it seem clear? What does the water look like in a glass jar? What does a drop of water look like under a microscope?

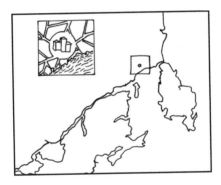

"Flight of Birds" questions

These are wide open questions that might not have any answer—questions generated from the non-rational as well as the rational mind. For example: What would the world be like without colors? Why do people love rainbows so much?

You can remind yourself to use these kinds of questions in the course of an ordinary school day by planning questions ahead of time or keeping the categories written on a card in front of you. You can go public with your desire to ask questions that might have many different answers and then follow through. And you can teach the children about the different kinds of questions and then challenge them to practice and use them.

And even if you don't make major changes in the way you incorporate questioning, at least some of the time—especially when things are getting a little dry and ordinary—ask a wondering question, such as, "How does a plant know just what shape flower to make? How come daisies don't make blue petals now and then?" And the children are off into the world of imagination where anything is possible.

Question bubbles

Cartooning is a playful art form that is useful in stimulating free-form question-asking and imagining. Students can be challenged to draw a figure (which can be based on a character in books, history, or current events, or just on a person from the child's imagination). The figure can ask any type of question, but the most energizing questions are open-ended—something the student artist wonders about or thinks his character might wonder about, something for which nobody really has the right answer. The drawn figures and their questions, written in speech bubbles, can be mounted in a display that invites viewers to give a try at an answer. Or students might incorporate the drawings and questions into wonder journals or other writing.

What we are seeking in this is a pedagogy of questions, not answers (although straightforward answers certainly have their place—just not *every* place). We're trying to develop a culture where asking becomes a habit and students begin to inquire freely and often—of the teacher, of each other, of themselves—about the edges and oddities as well as the obvious in life. They keep *wondering* about things. This kind of questioning goes beyond merely making art to thinking as an artist thinks, the kind of thinking that makes corporations hire people with an arts background because they are more likely to be creative, original problem solvers.

Breathing Out: Making Something from Nothing

One major US corporation uses a training program, *Creatrix,* that is specifically designed to nurture dreaming and innovation. In order to "break set," to fracture routine thinking, the executives do things they have never done before—make curtains, design a kitchen—so that they can experience themselves as risk-taking creators. (Cruz 2002)

The executives are using what the City Building Education™ approach to learning describes as Backward Thinking™, which starts with inventing new ways to do things, designing new ways for things to look, or predicting future variations for something already known. (California State Polytechnic University at Pomona 2004) In City Building Education, for example, students design a city or a house, using not only what they already know, but also their intuition and spontaneity.

*These simple drawings allow children
to explore visually the concept of equals.*

After the creating is done, the students go back and analyze their results: What worked? What didn't? Why or why not? Let's find out. Let's fix it.

The idea here—as with most work in the arts—is to arrive at breadth, depth, and originality through multiple points of view. To do this, students begin with the unknown rather than with already given or known right answers. What this suggests to me as a teacher is to *start* with student exploration and expression, and *then* teach my lesson from what they have created. Here are some examples:

I want my fifth graders to begin a study of equations.

Instead of starting with an already balanced equation, describing it, and providing a definition of equations in general, I will begin by asking students to make something that balances. I'll give them colored paper scraps, toothpicks, cubes, paper clips—whatever materials are easy to gather, to make this "thing" that balances. I'll allow them ten minutes. They can work in pairs. Afterwards, we'll circle up and discuss our examples of balance, translating the three-dimensional sculptures into a written equation.

For example, if two students make a seesaw out of a popsicle stick laid across a little block, with two pipe cleaner figures balancing at the ends, we can call the two pipe cleaner figures "A" and "B". The equation is "A = B". Balance occurs when there is equal weight on both sides of the seesaw. If we had two figures at one end and one at the other the sculpture would not balance. The equation for that would be "2A ≠ B". We can then ask the students, "What would it take to balance this equation?" Possibilities are "2A = 2B" or "A = B". We will *discover* equations by the end of a lesson that begins with open-ended messing around.

I want to teach my seventh graders about plant and animal classification.

Instead of presenting a chart showing all the kingdoms and phyla and species, I will begin by asking students to make up an animal—draw it and be ready to tell us how it breathes, eats, eliminates, and reproduces. I'll give them ten minutes. They can work in pairs. Afterwards we'll circle up and figure out together how to organize these animals: all those that lay eggs go together, all the ones with lungs together, etc. It doesn't really matter how the classifications go—what we want to experience is the sorting process by which plant and animal classification was done in the first place. And we want to have fun while we think, disagree, and explain.

I want second grade students to begin writing longer, more complex sentences.

Instead of beginning with examples of simple, compound, and complex sentences, I will ask each set of partners to write a sentence about balloons on a sentence strip. I give them five minutes. Then we circle up and someone picks two sentences from the strips now lying in the center of the circle or taped to the board. The challenge is for us to put these two sentences together into one more interesting and longer sentence. If things go as usual, we'll end up with a funny paragraph of well-structured sentences.

In each of these lessons we begin by creating something from nothing, a process both exciting and unbalancing. It sets up a classroom environment which calls for non-algorithmic thinking: First we want to hear what interests you and see what you have made, and then build from your original ideas. It will stretch those students whose learning preference (based perhaps on years of practice) is, "Tell me what to do, exactly how, and I'll do it." It will be liberation and motivation for those who crave opportunities for original thinking.

I worked with a boy who was an extraordinary storyteller. At various moments of the school day, he would have a few children around him to hear the latest episode of the endless saga he had invented. One day I looked out the window and saw him walking around the softball infield talking to himself during recess:

"What were you doing out there, Matt?"

"Telling my story."

"Why don't you write it down, so you will remember it?"

"I do remember it. I don't need to write it down."

He seemed to keep straight in his mind an amazingly long series of details about an amazingly long list of characters. The other children vouched for Matt. He never mixed things up, was always true to the original plot and characters. He was a natural, brilliant storyteller, and the chance to spin the story *out loud,* for himself and an audience, contributed greatly to his sense of well-being in school.

I finally got Matt to channel his remarkable gift for narrative into a writing project by giving him the opportunity to write, produce, and direct his own play. Although his play was a success, he continued to feel that the storytelling was what mattered most to him and where he put his best energy. He loved the free flow, the intensity, the mental captivation of making something from nothing for a live audience. In one meaning of the word, I thought of Matt as a genius, the meaning that goes back to the origins of "gen" as in the Greek "genea" (birth) or Latin "gignere" (to beget). It was as if Matt grew in his understanding of the world as he generated stories from his imagination. When we give students the chance to begin with creative exploration, we honor the genius in all of them.

Breathing Out: Playful Learning

There had better be some laughs along the way, too. Without the presence of play, learning becomes the dreary tedium of merely covering the curriculum. The possibility of the individual creative act is greatly reduced in the presence of unrelenting sobriety:

> Researchers report that when teams of people are working together on a problem, those groups that laugh most readily and most often (within limits—you can't goof off entirely) are more creative and productive than their more dour and decorous counterparts. Joking around makes good sense: playfulness is itself a creative state. (Goleman et al. 1992, 38)

But what about those of us who aren't good joke tellers and are too self-conscious for silliness? We can become magnets for those who are. Just as stories, images, and songs are necessary to our survival as whole beings, so is laughter. Look for the odd. Celebrate the offbeat. Cultivate some silliness every day. I don't mean sarcasm, that flesh-ripping substitute for humor that harms relationships and reduces safety in the classroom. I mean the kind of fun where nobody gets hurt:

- Read funny poems.

- Tell silly jokes. (*Why did the dinosaur cross the road? Because chickens weren't invented yet.*)

- Tell stories about your best mess-ups.

What has this got to do with art? Everything. Art is a way of being alive. It is that cockeyed wonder that we adore in toddlers, preserved in a grown-up. I have been lucky enough to live my life with people who are a little odd. I wish the same for you. Cultivate your idiosyncrasies. They will liberate you and the children—and who knows what wonderful ideas will come to light in your classroom?

The best compliment I ever received was from my seven-year-old granddaughter. Four of us were sitting around the kitchen table, and one of the children did something silly. We all laughed, and the two adults laughed the longest. "That's what I like about you two," Sylvie said. "The things kids think are funny, you think are funny too."

What I know about children is that laughing with them makes you feel like friends, breaks tensions, lifts everyone's spirits, and washes away crabbiness. Why wouldn't I laugh? Why don't we laugh every chance we get with our students? Considering the struggles—the poverty, the fear, the dangers and frustrations—of ordinary life, we need laughter the way we need air. It doesn't change anything, and it changes everything. It makes it possible for children to think well and work imaginatively.

But the value of play goes beyond telling jokes and laughing. Living and working in the world of imagination brings joy. The traditional Inuit knew that they could not sustain themselves in their unforgiving arctic environment without joy. Utitiaq's *Song* offers us lifesaving advice:

> *Aja*, I am joyful; this is good!
> *Aja*, there is nothing but ice around me, that is good!

Aja, I am joyful; this is good!
My country is nothing but slush, that is good!
Aja, I am joyful; this is good!
Aja, when, indeed, will this end? This is good!
I am tired of watching and waking, this is good!

(Lewis 1971, 113)

At Reggio Emilia, an early childhood center in northern Italy, teachers believe so much in the growth that children can achieve in an atmosphere of good spirits that they operate under the motto:

"Niente Senza Gioia"   "Nothing Without Joy" (Goleman et al 1982)

I believe that to live well in a rough world, our children need to play with their learning—to laugh, to wander and wonder, and to experience the deep release and pleasure of making stuff up.

Lively Learning

Do we have time for imaginative, artful thinking in school? Dare we allow students to cruise the side roads when all the days of the school year are insufficient to the task of covering the curriculum? As Duckworth reminds us, our job is to *uncover* the curriculum. (Duckworth 1996, 7) To do that, we'll have to let children think their own thoughts about their own experiences, and express them—at least some of the time—in their own ways.

There's a history of good things from people who sought the roads not traveled. Einstein, in search of the holy grail of a meaningful, single plan and purpose for life, stumbled upon the theory of relativity and told us about it. If we let our young folks engage in art-full learning each day, they may become just the kind of good thinkers we say we want them to be. To develop in our children the confidence and efficacy they need to flourish, let's offer them the gift of imagination, so that they can say:

Today is a day for learning. I am joyful. This is good.

WORKS CITED

Ashton-Warner, Sylvia. 1963. *Teacher.* New York: Bantam Books.

California State Polytechnic University. "City Building Education." http://www.csupomona.edu/~dnelson/cbe.html. Accessed January 2004.

Cruz, Sherri. 2002. "Unlocking Creativity." Minneapolis Star-Tribune (Nov 15).

Duckworth, Eleanor. 1996. *"The Having of Wonderful Ideas" and Other Essays on Teaching and Learning.* New York: Teachers College Press.

Feeney, Jon. 1963. *Eskimo Artist: Kenojuak. Documentary film.* Montreal: National Film Board of Canada.

Goleman, Daniel, Paul Kaufman, and Michael Ray. 1992. *The Creative Spirit.* New York: Dutton.

Lewis, Richard, ed. 1971. *I Breathe a New Song: Poems of the Eskimo.* New York: Simon & Schuster.

Resources
Creativity and Learning

Armstrong, Thomas. 1998. *Awakening Genius in the Classroom*. Alexandria, VA: Association for Supervision and Curriculum Development (ASCD).

> Describes twelve "genius qualities," such as curiosity, sensitivity, inventiveness, and joy, and offers classroom activities and resources to nurture these qualities.

Costa, Arthur L., and Bena Kallick, eds. 2000. *Discovering and Exploring Habits of Mind*. Alexandria, VA: Association for Supervision and Curriculum Development (ASCD).

> This is the first in a four book series, *Habits of Mind: A Developmental Series*. This book explores sixteen types of intelligent behaviors to cultivate in students.

Duckworth, Eleanor. 1996. *"The Having of Wonderful Ideas" and Other Essays on Teaching and Learning*. 2nd edition. New York: Teachers College Press.

> Duckworth writes about helping children construct their own understanding and invent ideas in various subject areas.

Goleman, Daniel, Paul Kaufman, and Michael Ray. 1992. *The Creative Spirit*. New York: Dutton.

> This companion book to the PBS television series explores the nature of creativity and offers ideas and practical exercises for cultivating creativity.

Goleman, Daniel. 1995. *Emotional Intelligence*. New York: Bantam Books.

> Draws on brain and behavioral research to make a strong case for the importance of emotional intelligence.

Smith, Frank. 1998. *The Book of Learning and Forgetting*. New York: Teachers College Press.

> Smith critiques the view that learning is hard work with a goal of achieving measurable mastery. Instead, he argues for the view that learning is an ongoing social process.

Wolfe, Patricia. 2001. *Brain Matters: Translating Research into Classroom Practice*. Alexandria, VA: Association for Supervision and Curriculum Development (ASCD).

> Wolfe offers concise information on brain research and its implications for the classroom. Includes information that supports arts-integration.

Drawing and Other Visual Arts

Beal, Nancy. 2001. *The Art of Teaching Art to Children in School and at Home*. New York: Farrar, Straus, and Giroux.

> A developmentally-based approach to teaching personal expression through collage, drawing, painting, clay, printmaking, and construction.

Brookes, Mona. 1996. *Drawing with Children: A Creative Method for Adult Beginners, Too.* Los Angeles: J. P. Tarcher.

> A revised and expanded edition of a popular, easy-to-follow approach to drawing for children and adults.

Cohen, Elaine Pear, and Ruth Straus Gainer. 1995. *Art: Another Language for Learning.* 3rd edition. Portsmouth, NH: Heinemann.

> Stories, examples, and discussions about the power of visual art to empower children.

Doris, Ellen. 1991. *Doing What Scientists Do: Children Learn to Investigate Their World.* Portsmouth, NH: Heinemann.

> Doris, a science teacher, approaches science as a process of discovery and makes science enjoyable and accessible for both students and teachers. Includes information on using observational drawing to teach the scientific method.

Edwards, Betty. 1989. *Drawing on the Right Side of the Brain: A Course in Enhancing Creativity and Artistic Confidence.* Los Angeles: J. P. Tarcher.

> Presents a method for learning to draw that starts with seeing the way an artist sees.

Ewald, Wendy, with Alexandra Lightfoot. 2001. *I Wanna Take Me a Picture: Teaching Photography and Writing to Children.* Boston: Beacon Press; Durham, NC: Center for Documentary Studies at Duke University.

> Provides a series of lessons to begin the development of children's photography skills.

Gee, Karolynne. 2001. *Visual Arts as a Way of Knowing.* Portland, ME: Stenhouse Publishers; Los Angeles: The Galef Institute.

> Part of the *Strategies for Teaching and Learning Professional Library,* this book provides exercises that help teach drawing, color, and design. Exercises are accompanied by teacher stories of integrating the arts into subject areas.

Richardson, Elwyn S. 1964. *In the Early World: Discovering Art Through Crafts.* New York: Pantheon Books.

> Richardson vividly evokes the science-arts connections he helped children make in his New Zealand classroom.

Tallarico, Tony. 1982. *The Giant I Can Draw Everything.* New York: Little Brown.

> Teachers can use these step-by-step sequences to help students draw people, animals, and objects.

Music

Music collections

Bernstein, Sara. 1994. *Hand Clap! "Miss Mary Mack" and 42 Other Hand-Clapping Games for Kids.* Avon, MA: Adams Media Corporation.

> Sara Bernstein was twelve years old when she put together this extensive collection. Grades K–8.

Dadson, Philip, and Don McGlashan. 1995. *The From Scratch Rhythm Workbook*. Revised edition. Portsmouth, NH: Heinemann.

> Presents a body-based approach to rhythm and sound that encourages group work and active participation. Grades K–8.

Davis, Andy, Peter Amidon, and Mary Alice Amidon, eds. 2000. *Down in the Valley: More Great Singing Games for Children*. Brattleboro, VT: New England Dancing Masters Productions.

> Songbook and CD set. Presents twenty-five singing games from a variety of traditions. Includes tips on teaching the games and bringing dancing into the classroom. Grades K–8. Available through www.dancingmasters.com

Feldman, Jean. 1995. *Transition Time: Let's Do Something Different!* Beltsville, MD: Gryphon House.

> Presents dozens of ideas for games, songs, and movement that help children transition through the day smoothly. Grades Pre-K–2.

Gilpatrick, Elizabeth. 1991. *'Round We Go! 40 New Rounds with Activities for Young Singers*. Van Nuys, CA: Alfred Publishing Co.

> A collection of original rounds that range from very simple two-part rounds to quite complex five- and seven-part rounds for older students. Grades K–6.

Kriete, Roxann, with contributions by Lynn Bechtel. 2001. *The Morning Meeting Book*. Greenfield, MA: Northeast Foundation for Children.

> Part of the *Strategies for Teachers* series. Includes appendices of greetings and group activities, many of which can be sung or chanted. Grades K–8.

Mattox, Cheryl Warren, ed. 1991. *Shake It to the One That You Love the Best: Play Songs and Lullabies from the Black Musical Tradition*. Illus. by Varnette Honeywood and Brenda Joysmith. Nashville, TN: JTG of Nashville.

> Available as a songbook and audiotape or CD set. Grades K–2.

Northeast Foundation for Children. 1998. *16 Songs Kids Love to Sing*. Greenfield, MA: Northeast Foundation for Children.

> Songbook and CD set. Sixteen of the favorite songs from Northeast Foundation for Children's summer workshops for teachers. Grades K–8.

Other music resources

The Children's Music Network™, P.O Box 1341, Evanston, IL 60204-1341, www.cmnonline.org

> A nonprofit association of people interested in children's music. Members share songs and ideas.

HIGH/SCOPE® Educational Research Foundation, 600 North River Street, Ypsilanti, MI 48198-2898, www.highscope.org

> High/Scope has extensive resources on using music in the classroom, particularly with primary grade children.

Movement

Amidon, Peter, Andy Davis, and Mary Cay Brass, eds. 1991. *Chimes of Dunkirk—Great Dances for Children.* Brattleboro, VT: New England Dancing Masters Productions.

> Available as book plus audiotape or CD. A collection of traditional dances. The audiotape and CD have dance-length music for each dance in the book. Available from www.dancingmasters.com

Chimes of Dunkirk - Teaching Dance to Children—the video. 2003. Produced by New England Dancing Masters and Country Dance and Song Society. Edited by Gerret Warner. Directed and narrated by Peter Amidon. 62 min. Available in DVD or VHS.

> Includes footage of eighteen dances, dance teaching and calling by experienced callers and elementary school teachers, and information on teaching traditional dance to children. Available from www.dancingmasters.com

Hagedorn, Elizabeth, and Sarah Lindquist. 2001. *Flexible Bodies, Flexible Minds: Integrating Dance and Mathematics Using the Everyday Mathematics Curriculum Grades 1–3, Volume 1.* Minneapolis: Minneapolis Public Schools Math Department.

Hagedorn, Elizabeth, Sarah Lindquist, Gretchen Pick, and Roxane Wallace. 2001. *Flexible Bodies, Flexible Minds: Integrating Dance and Mathematics Using the Everyday Mathematics Curriculum Grades 1–3, Volume 2.* Minneapolis: Minneapolis Public Schools Math Department.

> Detailed descriptions of successful math lessons that incorporate movement, written by classroom teachers who use them. To get copies of these two curricula, contact Joan Byhre, jbyhre@mpls.k12.mn.us. There is a small fee for copying and postage.

Hannaford, Carla. 1995. *Smart Moves: Why Learning Is Not All in your Head.* Arlington, VA: Great Ocean Publishers, Inc.

> Describes the body's role in thinking and learning, including an introduction to exercises that maintain balanced mind/body learning.

HIGH/SCOPE® Educational Research Foundation, 600 North River Street, Ypsilanti, MI 48198-2898, www.highscope.org

> High/Scope has extensive resources on using movement and dance in the classroom, particularly with primary grade children.

Jensen, Eric. 2000. *Learning with the Body in Mind: The Scientific Basis for Energizers, Movement, Play, Games, and Physical Education.* San Diego, CA: The Brain Store, Inc.

> Presents current research on the mind-body connection and considers the implications for learning. Includes practical strategies for using movement in the classroom.

Stewart, Mary, and Kathy Phillips. 1992. *Yoga for Children.* New York: Simon & Schuster.

> Stewart, an experienced yoga teacher, presents simple yoga movements and games. Includes photographs of children doing the poses as well as written directions.

Weikart, Phyllis S., and Elizabeth B. Carlton. 2002. *85 Engaging Movement Activities—Learning on the Move, K–6 Series.* Ypsilanti, MI: High/Scope Press.

> This book offers many ideas for challenging and enjoyable movement experiences that develop students' language abilities, vocabulary, concentration, planning skills, and cooperative decision making skills. Includes easy-to-follow plans for each activity.

Zakkai, Jennifer Donohue. 1997. *Dance As a Way of Knowing.* Portland, ME: Stenhouse Publishers; Los Angeles: The Galef Institute.

> Part of the *Strategies for Teaching and Learning Professional Library,* this book describes the elements of dance and gives model lessons for integrating movement into the curriculum.

Theater

Bany-Winters, Lisa. 1997. *On Stage: Theater Games and Activities for Kids.* Chicago: Chicago Review Press.

> Includes a wide variety of theater games grouped into categories such as improvisation, monologues, creating characters. Designed for use by children as well as grown-ups.

Collins, Rives, and Pamela J. Cooper. 1997. *The Power of Story: Teaching Through Storytelling.* 2nd edition. Scottsdale, AZ: Gorsuch Scarisbrick Publishers.

> The authors, one a storyteller and one a teacher, show how teaching through personal stories can bring drama into learning. Includes suggestions for successful storytelling.

Egan, Kieran. 1986. *Teaching as Story Telling: An Alternative Approach to Teaching and Curriculum in the Elementary School.* Chicago: The University of Chicago Press.

> In the introduction to this book, Egan describes his model as one "that encourages us to see lessons or units as good stories to be told…" The book provides a guide to using storytelling in teaching across the curriculum.

Origins. 1995. *The Immigrants—Simulations.* Minneapolis: Origins.

> Two simulations for exploring and understanding the immigration experience. Interview several fictional immigrants and enact a simulation of Ellis Island. Includes an interactive timeline, bibliography, and suggestions for extensions. Available from http://resources.originsonline.org/musicFolio.shtml

Paley, Vivian Gussin. 1999. *The Kindness of Children.* Cambridge, MA: Harvard University Press.

> Paley explores the kindness of children through their stories, as told to her and reenacted by them.

Peterson, Lenka, and Dan O'Connor. 1997. *Kids Take the Stage: Helping Young People Discover the Creative Outlet of Theater.* New York: Watson-Guptill Publications.

> A practical guide to teaching acting skills and directing plays with children.

Spolin, Viola. 1986. *Theater Games for the Classroom: A Teacher's Handbook.* Evanston, IL: Northwestern University Press.

> A classic presentation of theater exercises for the classroom, accompanied by practical advice that helps make them successful.

Poetry and Writing

Calkins, Lucy McCormick. 1986. *The Art of Teaching Writing.* Portsmouth, NH: Heinemann.

> A classic on helping children become authentic writers.

Christensen, Linda. 2000. *Reading, Writing, and Rising Up: Teaching About Social Justice and the Power of the Written Word.* Milwaukee, WI: Rethinking Schools Ltd.

> Presents techniques for using writing to help children explore issues of social justice and better understand themselves.

Collom, Jack. 1985. *Moving Windows: Evaluating the Poetry Children Write.* New York: Teachers and Writers Collaborative.

> This guide to evaluating student poetry helps teach children to write poems with authenticity and style.

Collom, Jack, and Sheryl Noethe. 1994. *Poetry Everywhere: Teaching Poetry Writing in School and in the Community.* New York: Teachers and Writers Collaborative.

> Sixty clear and specific exercises with plentiful examples of poetry by published writers and children.

Graves, Donald. 1992. *Explore Poetry.* Portsmouth, NH: Heinemann.

> Addresses both the reading and writing of poetry. Includes specific exercises as well as information about using poetry across the curriculum.

Magliaro, Elaine. *Mrs. Magliaro's Poetry Page.* Malcolm Bell School, Marblehead, MA. http://www.marblehead.com/staff/emagliar/poetry.htm#poetryacrosscurriculum

> Web page created by a school librarian provides extensive resources for using poetry in the classroom.

Padgett, Ron, ed. 2000. *Handbook of Poetic Forms.* 2nd edition. New York: Teachers and Writers Collaborative.

> An easy-to-use dictionary of over seventy poetic forms with descriptions and examples for each.

Poetry collections

Bierhorst, John. 1994. *On the Road of Stars: Native American Night Poems and Sleep Charms.* New York: Simon and Schuster.

> More than fifty poems from twenty-two tribal traditions. Grades 4–8.

Bruchac, Joseph. 1998. *The Earth Under Sky Bear's Feet: Native American Poems of the Land.* New York: Puffin.

> With the organizing device of a grandmother telling the story of Sky Bear to her grand-daughter, Bruchac presents twelve poems, each from a different Native American group. Grades K–5.

Cullinan, Bernice, ed. 1996. *A Jar of Tiny Stars: Poems by NCTE Award-Winning Poets.* Honesdale, PA: Wordsong/Boyds Mills Press.

> Children's favorite poems from ten NCTE award-winning poets. Grades K–6.

Fleischman, Paul. 1988. *Joyful Noise: Poems for Two Voices.* New York: HarperCollins.

> A collection of poems in the first person voices of different insects; designed to be read aloud by two voices. Grades K–6.

Hopkins, Lee Bennet, ed. 2002. *Home to Me: Poems Across America.* New York: Orchard Books.

> Hopkins asked fifteen poets from around the country to write poems about home. Grades K–5.

Keenan, Deborah, and Roseann Lloyd, eds. 1990. *Looking for Home: Women Writing About Exile.* Minneapolis: Milkweed Editions.

> Keenan and Lloyd, both poets, have collected poems by women, many of whom were born in other countries. An adult book that could be used in grades 5–8.

Nye, Naomi Shihab, ed. 1998. *The Space Between Our Footsteps: Poems and Paintings from the Middle East.* New York: Simon & Schuster.

> A collection of drawings and poems from nineteen middle Eastern countries. Grades 6–8 and above.

Prelutsky, Jack, ed. 1997. *The Beauty of the Beast: Poems from the Animal Kingdom.* New York: Knopf Books for Young Readers.

> 200 poems from 100 contemporary poets. Grades 1–6.

————————. 1983. *The Random House Book of Poetry for Children.* New York: Random House.

> 500 poems arranged thematically. Grades 1–6.

Strickland, Dorothy S., and Michael R. Strickland, eds. 1994. *Families: Poems Celebrating the African American Experience.* Honesdale, PA: Wordsong/Boyds Mills Press.

> Twenty-three poems about African American families. Grades K–3.

About the Author

Linda Crawford has been an educator for forty years, working at the pre-school through graduate school levels. She has taught English in high school, been an artist-in-residence in elementary and middle schools, taught multicultural understanding through the arts at all levels, and served as the principal of a K–5 elementary school. She is the director of Origins, a twenty-five-year-old nonprofit organization dedicated to community-building, especially through the arts.

Linda is the author of *To Hold Us Together: Seven Conversations for Multicultural Understanding* and editor of several multicultural exhibition catalogs and videos. She operated an art gallery and touring arts organization specializing in the contemporary art of the Inuit and other Native peoples. She lives in Minneapolis and plays with her grandchildren at every opportunity.

About Northeast Foundation for Children, Inc.

Northeast Foundation for Children, Inc. (NEFC) is a nonprofit educational organization whose mission is to foster safe, challenging, and joyful elementary classrooms and schools. NEFC develops and promotes the *Responsive Classroom*® approach to teaching, which offers educators practical strategies for bringing together social and academic learning throughout the school day.

NEFC offers workshops for teachers, a newsletter and website, books and other resources, and on-site services for schools and school districts.

For more information, please contact:

NORTHEAST FOUNDATION FOR CHILDREN, INC.
85 Avenue A, Suite 204, P.O. Box 718, Turners Falls, Massachusetts 01376
800-360-6332
www.responsiveclassroom.org

About Origins

Origins is a nonprofit educational organization that works with children, teachers, and parents to generate and nurture community support and academic success. Based in Minneapolis, Origins is a regional center for the *Responsive Classroom* approach.

Origins offers the workshop "Building Academic Communities Through the Arts," as well as workshops in the *Responsive Classroom* approach, a newsletter and website, and on-site consultation to schools.

Building Academic Communities Through the Arts (BACTA)

This book grew out of work done with teachers in the week-long summer workshop "Building Academic Communities Through the Arts," which helps teachers learn how to build a classroom community using arts-based teaching tools: drawing, storytelling, simulations, music, visual thinking skills, poetry, and movement.

For more information about Origins and the BACTA workshops, please contact:

Origins
3805 Grand Avenue South, Minneapolis, Minnesota 55409
800-543-8715
www.originsonline.org